Things That BITE

A REALISTIC LOOK AT CRITTERS THAT SCARE PEOPLE

by Tom Anderson

ADVENTURE PUBLICATIONS, INC.
CAMBRIDGE, MINNESOTA

To Nancy for your love, support and love bites.

Acknowledgments

In the summer of 1993, I was paddling on the upper reaches of the Seal River in northern Manitoba with author, guide and dear friend Cliff Jacobson. The bugs were bad and I jokingly suggested that Cliff write a book on the Basic Essentials of Things That Bite. He waved the mosquitoes from his face and said, "No Tom, that is a book you should write." Since that summer, not a year has passed where Cliff hasn't asked me about the book's progress. So thanks Cliff, for your urgings, support and confidence. I am hoping we can share more campfires in places where things bite.

This book would not have been possible without the input from naturalists, teachers and others in contact with people in the outdoors. Too numerous to name, you know who you are. Thank you Larry Weber, John Moriarity and Peggy Callahan for taking the time to answer pesky and likely bothersome questions. Special thanks to Michael L. Draney, Ph.D. (University of Wisconsin-Green Bay and Cofrin Center for Biodiversity) for reviewing the spider chapter.

Thanks to Gerri and Gordon Slabaugh of Adventure Publications for having faith in me and for really paying attention to my suggestions. Monica Ahlman and Dan Johnson at Adventure also made this project fun and easy to work on.

Thanks to family and dear friends, especially Britta, Blake, Maren, Mom, Orv, Nels, Kingsie for putting up with my time focused on the book. A day doesn't pass where I feel such gratitude to being married to the best editor, supporter, business partner, coach and play-mate in the whole world! Thanks Nancy, you are such a gift to me.

This book isn't possible without the wonderful host of critters that love to bite. Imagine a world without "things that bite!" Wait . . . without them we would likely be dead. Hail the complex web of biological diversity!

Edited by Dan Johnson
Cover and book design by Jonathan Norberg
Cartoon illustrations by Erik Ahlman and Brenna Slabaugh
All chapter introduction artwork by Julie Martinez

See page 139 for photo credits by photographer and page number.

10 9 8 7 6 5 4 3 2 1

Copyright 2008 by Tom Anderson
Published by Adventure Publications, Inc.
820 Cleveland Street South
Cambridge, MN 55008
1-800-678-7006
www.adventurepublications.net
Printed in China
ISBN-13: 978-1-59193-077-8
ISBN-10: 1-59193-077-4

Table of Contents

Aware, Not Afraid

*The last word in ignorance is the man who says of an animal or plant:
"What good is it?" If the land mechanism as a whole is good, then every part is
good, whether we understand it or not. If the biota, in the course of eons, has
built something we like but do not understand, then who but a fool would discard
seemingly useless parts? To keep every cog and wheel is the first precaution of
intelligent tinkering.*

-Aldo Leopold

Our nature, as humans, is to play favorites. Things that inflict pain or compete for our food or recreation tend to be labeled "bad." Those species that provide us with food or serve us in recreation, such as hunting and fishing, are conversely labeled as "good." Humans are the only species that judges the "goodness" or "badness" of other creatures.

I want to challenge the reader to marvel in the adaptations of the biters and stingers in this book. Each has a unique set of amazing adaptations, a genius in design and function. Each of the creatures featured plays an important role that benefits the whole system— including us. We should stand in wonder and awe of these beasts and in doing so come to know them and their places better.

The more we learn about something, the more we understand and respect it. It is doubtful that if you kill any of the stingers and biters that you will significantly impact their population. However, remember you have a choice, and they are not biting because they are "bad."

Each of us harbors fears. Research verifies that children learn many of their fears from adults, particularly their parents. A toddler who watches his parents cringe or overreact when a wasp flies near him, or when a spider or snake suddenly appears, will learn that such a response is normal. Children are not used to seeing their parents cringe in fear. This becomes an emotional bookmark in the child's life and is not easily forgotten. One of the best gifts you can give your child is to demonstrate curiosity and enthusiasm over the oddities (and yes, even the outcasts) of the animal world. This is a perfect opportunity to teach children respect, not fear.

This book is intended as a guide to animal species that might make an outing uncomfortable or painful. It is important to note that a few of them bite or sting as part of their strategy for obtaining food, but many species will bite or sting you only if they feel threatened or mishandled. For many of the creatures covered in this book, the customary way to deal with them is to quickly kill them. Besides there being ethical issues, some of them, like the gray wolf, are illegal to kill. Others, like black bears and raccoons, have seasons regulating when they can be harvested.

This book is also a guide to understanding the roles of the biters and stingers. It is my hope that the reader will learn that these particular creatures have many positive attributes that far outweigh the negative perspective. Not only will I introduce the reader to the basic natural history of the animal but I offer advice on how to avoid conflicts and if necessary how to treat a bite or sting.

Admittedly, I have not included every secret potion that is guaranteed to keep mosquitoes or deer flies away. There are always those long-held and honored family remedies that somehow don't get included in books like this. Sorry.

This book can accompany a trip to a state park, a picnic, a day on the trout stream, camping, canoeing or backpacking. It can make your fishing outing, backyard picnic or party more comfortable.

I owe a special thanks to the naturalists, federal and state park personnel, and outdoor recreationists who provided me with lists of critters that most commonly bother or concern them and—more importantly—the public at their respective center or park. This book, and particularly the list of "biters and stingers," would not have been possible without their input.

As a professional naturalist/author, I am an educator whose classroom is mostly the outdoors. I have had the good fortune of leading groups on various eco-trips throughout North America and into South America. Each area has its own unique assemblage of creatures, many of which can make your visit uncomfortable. Since this book deals with the Great Lakes Region, it does not make sense for me to introduce jellyfish, coral snakes or scorpions.

While honoring the fact that many people have fears and concerns about the species in this book, I can assure you it is highly unlikely you will ever be injured by a wolf, bear, coyote, skunk, raccoon, bat, garter snake, sunfish or muskie! These were added primarily to dispel myths and unfounded fears.

In the Great Lakes region, by far the most deadly of the creatures covered in this book are honeybees. Approximately 50 people die each year in the U.S. from bee/wasp/hornet stings (the bee delivers the most toxic venom), while an average of one person is killed each year in a large wild mammal attack.

yellowjacket

To put things in perspective I visited with a doctor in a hospital emergency room. I asked, "Of all the bites you deal with, which bites give you the greatest concern?" Almost immediately he responded, "Humans."

"Certainly," he added, "we sometimes have to deal with disfiguring dog bites, but the ones that invariably lead to nasty infections are those delivered by humans." It turns out that between our teeth legions of nasty anaerobic bacteria thrive. Each of us can tolerate our own bacteria, but not someone else's.

Another reality check is the fact that humans attack and kill their own fellow humans at a rate over 90,000 times that of bears attacking us.

Pogo, the infamous cartoon character of the 1960s and 1970s, perhaps put it best when he said, "We have met the enemy . . . and he is us."

My hope is this book will encourage you to explore the outdoors armed with a little more knowledge and with tips to make your experience more comfortable and pleasant. To get a better appreciation of the natural world and its role in our lives, we absolutely need the intimate connection of getting out there.

Enjoy the outdoors, aware—not afraid!

Tom

Anaphylactic Shock, Rabies and A Dose of Reality

The majority of the time, the most pain you will feel from a bite or a sting will likely be temporary. The likelihood of being bitten by a rabid mammal or experiencing a severe allergic reaction to a sting is small. However, you need to be observant and aware of the biter/stinger. The following information is intended to educate the reader about anaphylactic shock and rabies.

Anaphylaxis is a serious allergic reaction resulting from an insect sting, a bug bite or from exposure to food or drug allergens. Anaphylactic shock is the condition which can result from anaphylaxis, if left untreated. Rabies is a life-threatening virus which attacks the central nervous system.

Having some background and knowledge of these two uncommon afflictions will make your outdoor experience more comfortable. The irony is that the likelihood of being injured or killed when traveling by automobile or bicycle to your favorite beach or park is far greater than the probability of coming down with either rabies or anaphylactic shock. Keep things in perspective.

ANAPHYLAXIS

Anaphylaxis is a severe, potentially life-threatening allergic reaction. It can be caused by an insect bite or sting, as well as food or drug allergies. Development of the following signs and symptoms within minutes of exposure to a bite or sting is a strong indication of anaphylaxis:

- Constriction of the airways that results in difficulty breathing
- Shock associated with a severe decrease in blood pressure
- Weak and rapid pulse
- Confusion or anxiety
- Dizziness or fainting
- Hives and itching
- Flushed or pale skin
- Nausea, vomiting or diarrhea

If you've had anaphylaxis or have a history of allergies or asthma, you may have a greater chance of having an anaphylactic reaction. Ask your doctor about obtaining an Anaphylaxis Emergency Treatment Kit or an EpiPen. Both contain injectable adrenaline (epinephrine) for allergic reactions.

RABIES

Rabies is a viral disease that invades the central nervous system of mammals, including humans. The virus is commonly transmitted in saliva, when an infected animal bites another animal or person.

- The origin of the word rabies comes from the Latin word *rabere* which means "to rave or rage."

- Globally, more than 30,000 people die of rabies each year. Dogs are responsible for 99% of those deaths. Fortunately, few rabies deaths occur in the United States due to successful pet vaccination efforts.

- In the Great Lakes region, rabies most commonly occurs in bats, skunks, foxes and raccoons. There have been isolated cases in sheep, cats and cows.

- Most recent cases of rabies in humans in the United States have occurred after being bitten by an infected bat. (Reality check: It is estimated that less than 1% of bats carry rabies.) However, bats are rarely the cause of a rabies outbreak. They generally transmit the virus to other bats.

- In most areas where rabies outbreaks occur, the virus strain is traced back to dogs, cats, raccoons, skunks or other animals.

- After receiving an infectious bite it takes anywhere from 20 to 60 days for the virus to reach your brain. Early symptoms might be subtle. These could include headache, sore throat, fatigue or fever.

- Treatment for rabies is no longer the horror story we used to hear about. You know, multiple shots in your belly. You will initially receive a shot of human rabies immune globulin (HRIG) near the site of the bite. The following series of five vaccination shots will be in the upper arm.

- If you get bit by an animal and are unable to have the biting animal tested for rabies, you absolutely need to receive the rabies shots.

- Untreated, the rabies virus is fatal 100% of the time!

- The best prevention is to not handle or touch wild mammals. Don't be tempted to help a sick looking animal. Seek out help from properly trained wildlife professionals.

Swimmer's Itch

Remember the scene in the thriller movie *Jaws* when a shark attack sends scores of people fleeing the water for the safety of the beach? While we don't have sharks in our inland lakes, the same response is more quietly evident at many popular beaches. All it takes is for word to get out that swimmer's itch is afoot and the beach front can turn very lonely and quiet for some time.

Though the sky and water are blue and serene, there sometimes lurks beneath the calm surface a microscopic parasite capable of turning a pleasant day into a miserable, itching experience.

About Swimmer's Itch

Swimmer's itch, also called cercarial dermatitis, is a condition found throughout the United States. However, it is most common in the northern tier of states, such as those in the Great Lakes region.

Swimmer's itch is an allergic reaction caused by the aquatic larval stage of a group of flatworms called "schistosomes." Sneaky and small, they are approximately $1/80$ of an inch long and transparent. The rash and accompanying itch are responses swimmers and waders have after the free-swimming, microscopic parasites burrow into their skin.

Life and Times . . .

To understand the flatworm's complex life cycle, you need to know that a parasite depends on a host to feed on to develop. In the case of swimmer's itch, the unlucky sources of nourishment include snails (intermediate hosts) and birds (final hosts)—particularly water birds.

The adult parasite lives in the blood of infected animals such as ducks (particularly mergansers), gulls, herons and certain aquatic mammals such as muskrats and beavers.

male (left) and female mergansers

Inside the host animal, the parasite produces eggs that eventually make their way into the host's digestive system and are then passed in its feces. If the feces land in a body of water, the eggs usually hatch within an hour.

The hatched parasite is called the "miracidium." It is free-swimming, does not feed, and has enough energy for about a day's worth of host-hunting. The miracidium seeks out a specific type of snail and enters it. Over the period of about a month inside the snail, the parasite produces two more stages.

The final stage, called the cercaria, will burrow out of the snail. This is also a nonfeeding stage, but it must find a new host—most often a bird—within an hour or so. It does this by burrowing into the bird's skin or being swallowed by it. The parasite then enters the bird's blood stream and migrates through various organs before maturing. The adult flatworms living in the bird's blood stream produce great numbers of eggs, which are passed on in the bird's feces. And so the cycle repeats itself.

Fascinating Facts

- Some people do not get swimmer's itch. Approximately 30–40% of the population is sensitive to the infection. However, swimmer's itch is kind of like poison ivy in that every time you are exposed to the parasite, your sensitivity will increase and the reaction will be more intense.

- There are approximately 15 different species of schistosomes in the Great Lakes region. Most use only one species of snail and one species of bird to complete their life cycle.

- Of all water birds, it appears that the common merganser, a fish-eating duck, has the highest incidence of carrying the parasite.

Thanks to Swimmer's Itch

- Flatworms, like other parasites, are a sign of a healthy and diverse natural world.

- I am unaware of any benefits of this parasite other than those hosts that are able to cope with the parasite are likely to pass on those "coping genes" to their offspring. In a sense, it could be argued that the parasite helps to strengthen the host's bloodline.

Myth Busters

MYTH: You should always wear latex or rubber gloves when applying an itch-relieving cream on another person.

Swimmer's itch is not contagious and cannot be spread from one person to another. Gloves and other precautions are unnecessary.

Why They Bite

The parasitic larval flukes are simply trying to find a suitable host to complete their life cycle. It is simply a case of mistaken identity when they choose our skin instead of a particular aquatic bird or mammal.

How They Bite

When the cercari leaves the snail, it swims around looking for its next host. A pair of bare-skinned human legs wading in shallow water might be targeted. Humans, however, are not suitable hosts. Once the larvae burrow into our skin, they are unable to develop and they soon die.

How Afraid Should I Be?

Invading cercari are quickly detected and controlled by our immune systems, so they are not a life-threatening problem. And remember, these irritating parasites cannot complete their life cycles in the human body. The typical person's reaction is a rash and itching, usually lasting no more than a week.

Children are particularly susceptible to swimmer's itch since they spend more time in shallow water where the parasites are more likely to be found.

Symptoms show up quickly, sometimes within minutes of swimming in infected water. These include the following signs:

- burning or itching of the skin
- small reddish pimples and blisters

Preventing Swimmer's Itch

We cannot get rid of these parasites but we can reduce our exposure to them.

- Short and frequent dips into the water are better than a longer swim. The longer you are in the lake, the greater the chance of a parasite attaching itself to you.

- Avoid swimming near snail beds.

- Avoid swimming in the afternoon and early evening, when parasite concentrations are at their highest point of the day.

- Parasites prefer shallow water, so when possible avoid the shallows and swim in deeper water. This is not practical with non-swimmers such as young children.

- When coming out of the water, briskly and aggressively rub yourself off with a towel.

- Discourage ducks and geese from feeding or loafing around swimming areas.

- Copper sulfate is sometimes applied to the water to kill the snails, therefore breaking a vital link in the parasite's life cycle. However, there appears to be less use of this method in recent years due to concerns about the unknown effects that copper sulfate might have on aquatic ecosystems, and the results are often unpredictable.

THINK TWICE

Think twice about aggressively scratching the rash caused by swimmer's itch. Doing so could cause a more severe secondary infection.

Think twice about venturing into lakes or marshy areas with an abundance of snails. The higher the number of snails, the greater your chance of getting swimmer's itch.

NOTE: Dealing with pesticides and other chemicals in waterways is likely illegal in your area. Check with your state department of natural resources.

Treatment of Swimmer's Itch

- Apply cool compresses to the affected areas.

- Use corticosteroid cream.

- Bathe in Epsom salts or baking soda.

- Apply baking soda paste to the rash (made by stirring water into baking soda until it reaches a paste-like consistency).

- Use an anti-itch lotion or cream, such as Calamine lotion or Ken-tox.

- While most cases do not require medical attention, it's smart to see your doctor if a serious infection develops.

BOTTOM LINE

Swimmer's itch is not contagious and cannot be spread from one person to another. It is not a disease. It is caused by a parasite which, like other parasites, is a sign of a healthy natural world. And, although it causes some discomfort, the symptoms usually last no more than a week.

No-See-Ums

Despite their small size, these little gnats can drive people crazy and into the nearest shelter. I have known folks to pack up their tents, hook up their trailers and leave spectacular campgrounds to avoid a major hatch of no-see-ums.

No-see-ums can inflict misery simply by their legion numbers. Sometimes swarms are so thick that they are easily taken into our mouths, noses, eyes and ears.

About No-See-Ums

These little insects fall into a group known as biting midges, also known as "punkies" and no-see-ums. There are more than 100 species in North America. When these little flying insurgents are bad they can be worse than mosquitoes since they can easily infiltrate the average window screen.

Life and Times . . .

Like other flies, these tiny biters go through a complete metamorphosis. They go from egg to larva to pupa before finally reaching adulthood. This complex life cycle can take 2–6 weeks.

After ingesting a blood meal, the female seeks the edge of a wetland, where she lays her eggs on moist soil or mud. Some species can produce up to 450 eggs per batch. Eggs generally hatch within 2–10 days. The adult female will only live a few weeks.

The tiny, legless aquatic larvae scavenge on decaying organic matter in mud, sand, tree holes, water and vegetation. Species found in the Great Lakes region spend the winter in a dormant state in their larval stage and pupate in the spring before "emerging" as adults.

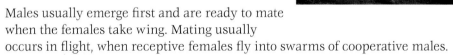

Males usually emerge first and are ready to mate when the females take wing. Mating usually occurs in flight, when receptive females fly into swarms of cooperative males.

Fascinating Facts

- No-see-ums belong to the order of "true flies" or *Diptera*, meaning two (*Di*) wings (*ptera*). There are more than 3,500 species in North America.

- While there are currently no issues with no-see-ums transmitting diseases to humans in the Great Lakes area, they are blamed for spreading bluetongue (a serious disease in ruminants such as sheep and cattle) among livestock in parts of the United States.

Thanks to No-See-Ums

- No-see-ums are very important in the food chain

- Many species of insects and fish that feed on the larvae, pupae and adult insects.

- These tiny insects, particularly the nectar-seeking males, are important plant pollinators.

Myth Busters

MYTH: The female no-see-um dies after one egg-laying episode.

Females are capable of laying several batches of eggs.

Why They Bite

Male no-see-ums do not bite. But the female needs a protein-rich blood meal in order to produce her eggs. She obtains it by biting a variety of involuntary donors such as reptiles, amphibians, birds and mammals—including humans.

THINK TWICE

Think twice about where you hike, picnic or set up camp. No-see-ums tend to stay in the vicinity of their wetland breeding grounds. Avoid these areas, particularly at dawn and dusk when these insects are most active.

Think twice about leaving your porch light on. No-see-ums are attracted to lights.

How They Bite

Like other biting flies, the female no-see-um has a tiny set of sharp mandibles or jaws that are used to cut into flesh. To help her quickly secure a blood meal, a natural blood thinner in her saliva makes it easier for her to suck up the blood.

The non-venomous bite in itself is not exceedingly painful. However, after the bite has been dealt, the itching and discomfort can be miserable.

How Afraid Should I Be?

Other than temporary discomfort, there is little reason to worry. Small, raised welts and blisters can form and last for several days. The greatest concern is that sometimes an allergic reaction can occur. Such a reaction will usually show up resembling a skin rash or infection.

Preventing No-See-Um Bites

- The simplest protection to prevent bites is to wear protective clothing (long pants and long-sleeved shirts).

- Insect repellants containing DEET help reduce the likelihood of bites.

- Since their small size allows them to crawl through the conventional 16-mesh wire screen, a finer mesh might be required to keep them outdoors.

- These tiny flies are weak fliers, so indoor fans set at high speeds can be used to keep the insects out of small areas.

- Some people have good luck with a spray-on sunscreen (SPF 30). Although it is DEET-free, it is recommended that you shower it off each night.

Treatment of Bites

- Clean the bites with soap and water.

- Itching and swelling can be reduced with the help of anti-itch and anti-inflammatory lotions and creams.

- Aspirin or Tylenol might offer additional relief. Do not administer aspirin to children under 15 years old.

- If blisters occur, apply an antibacterial/antibiotic ointment and keep the blisters loosely covered to allow air passage to help dry them out.

BOTTOM LINE

Protective clothing and other simple precautions will keep most no-see-ums at bay. But other than a little temporary discomfort, there is no reason to fear them. Their bite is neither venomous nor very painful. And although the itching and welts can be miserable, the discomfort is typically short-lived.

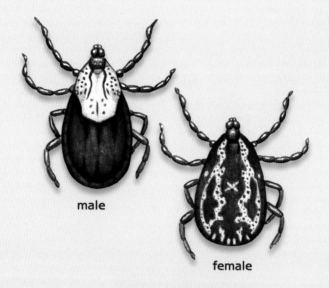

male

female

Ticks

Casually ask someone, "Is that a tick on your arm?" and you will likely witness an immediate and urgent response. For such a little fellow—no bigger than one of these typed letters—the tick easily motivates even the most macho of men into defensive action. And even after the hitchhiking tick is pointed out, there is a predictable, contagious outbreak among nearby people of twitching, scratching and subtle probing under their clothes.

Such is the power of this little creature.

About Ticks

Ticks are not insects. Like spiders, mites and scorpions, they are arachnids. Adult ticks have eight legs, while the larvae have six legs.

dog or wood tick   black-legged or deer tick

The two primary ticks of the Great Lakes region are the dog tick—also called wood tick—and the black-legged tick, commonly known as the deer tick. The smaller, black-legged tick is responsible for transmitting Lyme disease and other less-common tick-borne diseases such as human anaplasmosis.

The dog tick is the larger of the two, approximately ¼ inch in length. The female has a cream-colored disk behind her head, while the male lacks the disk and has two thin, light-colored stripes running down his back.

Unlike wood ticks, black-legged ticks have no white or cream-colored markings on their backs. They are about ⅛ inch long and darker (dark brown to black). Females usually have an area behind their head that is orange to red in color.

Life and Times . . .

Under ideal conditions, ticks have a two-year life cycle that includes blood-feeding stages as larvae, nymphs and adults.

In the spring, tick eggs hatch and tiny larval ticks emerge. Sometimes referred to as "seed ticks," they typically feed on the blood of small rodents such as mice. After developing into nymphs, they feed on small to medium-sized mammals such as chipmunks. Adults seek out larger animals, including white-tailed deer. Because deer are important hosts for female ticks securing blood meals for egg production, they play a key role in maintaining high tick populations.

In the Great Lakes region, the highest risk period for humans is May through August, when ticks are in the nymph stage. However there is also a chance of being bitten by adult ticks, so caution is advised from April through December.

Fascinating Facts

- Ticks have been reported to feed on at least 125 different animals—including 57 types of birds, 14 lizards and 54 mammal species.

- The folds in a tick's skin allow it to greatly expand in size. A "hungry" female might increase her weight by 200 times!

Thanks to Ticks

- Many species of birds feed on ticks, making them an important part of the food chain.

Myth Busters

MYTH: Ticks will leap out of trees onto you!

Ticks are crawlers, not jumpers. Leaping insects such as crickets or grasshoppers have longer, larger legs. The tiny legs of ticks are better suited for climbing up to ambush sites, from which they can lie in wait for a possible host to pass by.

Why They Bite

Simply put, ticks bite only to secure a meal. They require blood meals to change from one life stage to the next. A blood meal is also required by the adult female tick to produce her thousands of eggs.

electron microsope image of dog tick mouth

How They Bite

An electron microscope image of tick's mouthparts is reminiscent of the intergalactic aliens portrayed in the *Star Wars* movies. Creepy!

The tick's beak-like mouthpart has backward-pointing barbs that allow the tick to remain anchored for a successful bloodletting. After attaching themselves they secrete a protein-rich cementing substance that helps keep them in place. This patch of cement, which resembles a small chunk of your skin, can often be seen when a tick is removed.

As the tick feeds, it releases saliva containing special compounds that thin the blood and suppress pain.

How Afraid Should I Be?

Tick bites can cause some discomfort, such as itching or a rash, but alone they are not a major threat. However, in the past 25 years, ticks have taken on a new level in concern since they have been found to carry serious diseases.

The incidence of tick-borne illnesses, particularly Lyme disease, continue to increase in the Great Lakes region. Lyme disease is a bacterial infection caused by the bite of an infected tick. Left untreated, it can affect the skin, joints, heart and nervous system. The earlier the prescribed medical treatment of antibiotics is administered, the greater the likelihood of successful recovery.

THINK TWICE

Think twice before letting your dog indoors without a good tick check after a romp afield during tick season. Neglecting your pet might give ticks a free ride into your home.

Lyme disease is caused by a bacterium called a "spirochete" (spy-row-keete). The only way the spirochete can be transmitted to a host, such as a human, is for the tick to be attached for more than 48 hours—the time that experts deem long enough to transfer the bacterium into the host's blood stream.

Simply put, the longer a tick feeds on you, the greater the odds of it transmitting a tick-borne illness such as Lyme disease.

Preventing Tick Bites

The best ways to avoid tick bites include the following steps:

- Prevent them from getting to your skin.
- Perform diligent tick checks after outings. If appropriate, ask for help in checking hard-to-see spots such as your back.
- Limit your time in tall grass and brushy areas, particularly in the spring and fall.

- Wear long pants with the cuffs tucked into shin-high socks or boots. Light-colored clothing makes it easier to spot a hitchhiking tick.

- Chemical warfare on ticks can help. A 0.5% concentration of Permethrin sprayed on your pants and shirts can be very effective. Note it is important that you NOT spray Permethrin on your skin. Some folks claim that spraying a mosquito repellent with a high concentration of DEET on their clothes also repels ticks.

So you find a fastened tick. Now what?

- Immediate tick removal lessens the risk of infection.

- To properly remove a tick it is best to grasp it with a fine tweezers, but fingers will do the job. Do not us petroleum jelly, gasoline, nail polish remover or a hot match.

- Grasp the tick as close to the point of attachment as possible and pull straight up, gently but firmly. Do not jerk or twist the tick.

- Do not squeeze or crush the tick since that might push infectious substances into the wound.

- Don't worry if the tick's mouthparts remain in the skin. Your body will reject the foreign material and be rid of it in a few days. The bite might become reddish and even warm to the touch, but that's a normal reaction to rejecting a foreign body. It's kind of like getting a wood sliver.

electron microsope image of dog tick

- After the tick is removed, disinfect the skin thoroughly and wash your hands with soap and water.

- While it might be difficult to determine how long the tick has been fastened, it will help if you recall a situation when you might have picked up a tick. (Such as a hike in the woods, camping or petting a dog that has recently been outdoors.) This information will be particularly helpful should you later require medical treatment.

Treatment of Bites

- Seventy to 90% of Lyme-infected patients develop a circular, red "bull's-eye" rash at the site of the bite.

- Watch the bite site for a possible secondary infection or infectious rash for up to 30 days.

- Untreated, the infection might spread to other parts of your body within days or weeks. Symptoms could include fatigue, chills, fever, headache, muscle and joint aches and swollen lymph nodes.

- Left untreated, severe joint pain occurs in over half of the cases.

- Seek medical help for proper diagnosis of Lyme disease if you feel uneasy about a tick bite.

- If you find an engorged tick in your home, it has already fed on blood. If you do not have pets, the tick likely fed on you or other family members, and you should consult a doctor.

- As we continue to learn about Lyme disease and its treatment, there are ongoing questions and even controversy as to proper treatment. Your best defense is to watch for ticks and for unfolding knowledge on the subject.

BOTTOM LINE

Tick bites can cause mild discomfort, itching or a rash, but by themselves are not a major threat to human health. Although tick-borne diseases such as Lyme disease are a growing concern, an infected tick must be attached for more than 48 hours to transmit the disease. Preventative measures and frequent "tick checks" can greatly reduce your risk.

Black Flies

I recall a particularly memorable day of fishing brook trout in northern Minnesota when I had plenty of company on the water. Even though I finished the trip early so I could attend an evening wedding, I wore 42 black fly welts to the marriage ceremony. Yes, I really counted them.

A popular fishing fly, "the black gnat" is named after this blood-thirsty insect. Perhaps there is some sort of justice that this fly can be successfully used to catch "trout that bite!"

About Black Flies

Of the approximately 150 species of black flies in North America, some are fierce biters. Other non-biting black flies are simply a nuisance as they swarm around your face.

It hardly seems fair that such a small creature can cause so much misery. Stealthier than a mosquito's high-pitched whine, black flies swoop in for a meal of blood without even pricking us. They have tiny mandibles and in essence cut into our exposed flesh.

Life and Times . . .

Like mosquitoes, deer flies and horse flies, black flies begin life underwater. Female black flies lay their tiny cream-colored eggs at sunset on the water's surface or on wet vegetation along the shoreline. Each lays 200–800 eggs, which become attached to stones, sticks or vegetation in shallow, fast-running creeks, streams and rivers.

After hatching, the black or brown-colored larvae anchor themselves to rocks, sunken branches and other underwater objects. They filter microscopic food particles with their fine, brush-like mouthparts as the current flows by them. The larvae are sometimes so abundant and concentrated that they look like underwater moss. This stage lasts 6–7 months (usually over the winter).

A silken cocoon that is attached to underwater objects with small hook-like appendages covers the pupa. They can move by using silk and loops; almost like an underwater mountaineer. The cocoons look like slipper-shaped silk cases, attached to the bottom by the "toe" of the slipper, with the opening floating downstream. Even after the fly emerges from the stream, these empty "slipper" cases can be seen underwater.

Upon surfacing, it immediately flies to nearby vegetation, where its body hardens. (Insects, unlike us, have an exoskeleton—on the outside of their body.) After emerging, most black flies live 2–3 weeks, though some "long-lived" varieties survive up to 85 days.

Fascinating Facts

- Only female black flies bite.

- After pupating in the stream, an emerging black fly rides to the surface in a tiny bubble of air.

- Amazingly, hordes of black flies all hatch in the same time period.

- Their sheer numbers make them a threat to livestock, wildlife and humans. In the Far North, the black fly hatch often contributes to the movements of caribou and impacts the survival of caribou calves.

Thanks to Black Flies

- The aquatic larvae provide a food source for many species of fish.

- Birds and insects such as dragonflies feed on adult black flies.

- The male black fly feeds on flower nectar and is an important plant pollinator.

Myth Busters

MYTH: Large swarms of black flies swirling along a river or stream are very dangerous.

Though they look intimidating, these swarms are made up of non-biting males. The female, when ready to mate, flies into the swarm to find a willing male.

Why They Bite

Like their bloodletting mosquito neighbor, it is only the female black fly that must get a blood meal to assure the next generation. But unlike mosquitoes, which are most active at twilight and night, black flies are daytime biters and prefer low wind conditions. Luckily, black flies are only a nuisance in the Great Lakes Region for about three weeks, primarily in late May and June.

How They Bite

The female feeds from the mini-pool of blood in the hole she carves with her cutting bite. Her saliva contains anticoagulants—blood thinners—which make it easier to feed. These are the reason that the bite continues to bleed after she leaves, and are believed to cause allergic reactions. It's another case where, as with the mosquito, insect "spit" can make for an uncomfortable outing.

How Afraid Should I Be?

The bite first appears as a small red spot that might become slightly swollen. It then becomes itchy, irritating and more swollen. This reaction can last several days.

black fly

With multiple bites, itching is sometimes accompanied by an allergic reaction. Though not life threatening, it can cause mild to severe symptoms in sensitive individuals. A strong reaction might produce fever, nausea and allergic dermatitis.

Children are particularly vulnerable to black flies and may experience far more bites than an adults who are outdoors in the same area.

Preventing Black Fly Bites

PHYSICAL BARRIERS

- The easiest way to avoid black fly bites is to avoid areas around swift-flowing streams during late May and June. However, that is unreasonable for most of us, since this is a lovely time to be outdoors.

- Since black flies are daytime feeders, scheduling outings for evenings and nighttime will lessen your contact with them.

- Avoid perfumes and colognes. Black flies are also attracted to perspiration.

- Don't wear dark-colored clothing. Wearing light-colored, loose-fitting clothing really does help.

- If flies are numerous, a head net or bug jacket is essential. These small insects are persistent and will squeeze through any opening in your clothes, including slight gaps at pants cuffs, the belt line and shirtsleeves.

THINK TWICE

Think twice before camping next to that beautiful rushing stream in early summer. It's a prime breeding ground for black flies.

Think twice about wearing your favorite dark blue windbreaker when hiking or camping in black fly country in early summer. Go with light-colored clothing instead.

CHEMICAL REPELLENTS

Bug repellents are not very effective on black flies. If you choose to use them, use those with DEET. However, there are many who feel that wearing DEET might actually attract more black flies.

OTHER TRICKS IN OUTWITTING BLACK FLIES

- Sew a strip of Velcro on the sleeve openings of long-sleeved shirts to seal out black flies.

- Use large rubber bands around your pants cuffs to close off entry to your legs. (I have also tucked my pants into the tops of my socks.)

Treatment of Bites

- Wash the bites with warm water and soap. Relieve itching with products such as Benadryl and other anti-itching compounds and anti-inflammatory lotions and creams.

- If an allergic reaction occurs, seek immediate medical treatment.

BOTTOM LINE

A black fly's bite can produce a welt, but the reaction only lasts a few days. And despite their taste for blood, these little biters aren't all bad. At various life stages they provide food for fish, birds and dragonflies. Plus, the male is an important pollinator of many species of plants.

Mosquitoes

According to the Thompson River Indians of North America, Thunder asked Mosquito why he was so fat, and Mosquito replied that he sucked on trees. He didn't want to admit that he really fed on people, because he didn't want Thunder to eat up all the people and deny him of his prey. Mosquito's plan worked very well, and his story explains why Thunder now shoots trees instead of people.

About Mosquitoes

Although the Great Lakes region is home to only around 50 of the 2,500-plus species of mosquitoes found in the world, they are easily one of the most abundant "biters" you may encounter outdoors. Taken alone, a single mosquito doesn't seem all that intimidating. But what the mosquito lacks in stature, it makes up for in numbers and fearless tenacity. Swarms of droning mosquitoes have chased countless picnickers and campers from the woods, and even driven wanted criminals out of hiding. Fortunately, there's no need to let them ruin your outdoor adventures.

Life and Times . . .

Mosquitoes (*Culex species*) are members of the order Diptera. Considered "true flies," they are related to house flies and midges. Mosquitoes have two scaled wings, six long legs and, of course, a long, piercing proboscis (or beak).

Female mosquitoes lay 200–400 eggs in quiet marshes, swamps, ponds and other places which hold stagnant water like ditches, old tires and hoof prints. The eggs hatch within days of being laid. The tiny larvae hangs upside down like a letter "J" at the surface of the water. It feeds almost continuously on microscopic plant fragments.

About a dozen days later the larvae changes (pupates) into the adult mosquito. The pupa begins to fill its pupal covering with air until the skin splits open and out emerges the wobbly adult mosquito. It stands, resting, on the surface of its watery home for about a half an hour before it flies up to nearby grasses or brush.

Fascinating Facts

- Only female mosquitoes bite.

- Male mosquitoes feed on nectars from flowers or rotting fruit.

- The female's wings beat 250–500 times per second; the male's elaborate, feathery antennae helps him pick up their species-specific frequency and pitch.

- Mosquitoes are capable of mating within two days of hatching.

- A female mosquito mates only once in her life. She will receive all the sperm needed to produce up to 400 eggs.

Thanks to Mosquitoes

- Mosquitoes are a major plant pollinator in the Great Lakes region.

- Their larvae voraciously process tons of rotting plants (detritus) in a wetland.

- Mosquitoes are a main food source for other insects and wildlife such as ducklings and young fish. A single little brown bat may eat 5,000 mosquitoes in one night!

Myth Busters

MYTH: All mosquitoes are alike and can be controlled the same way.

There are more than 160 mosquito species in North America alone, and different species exhibit different behaviors. Some feed just before nightfall, others around the clock or whenever a host is near. Spraying of the winged, adult mosquitoes should be timed to reach these insects when they are flying and when the wind, humidity and general climate conditions favor targeting them.

MYTH: ZZZZZZZZAP!

Researchers found that while ultraviolet or black light "bug zappers" do attract and kill thousands of insects within a 24-hour period, mosquitoes comprise only 6.4% of a five-day insect catch. Of that, only half of the mosquitoes killed were the blood-feeding females. This is clearly not a good choice for controlling mosquitoes.

MYTH: The mosquito dies after she takes a blood meal.

Mosquitoes are capable of biting more than once. After the female mosquito takes a blood meal she completes the development of her eggs and may deposit up to 200 of them at a time. She may seek another blood meal and lay again.

Why They Bite

Proteins in the blood of warm-blooded animals are required to produce eggs, assuring there will be future generations of mosquitoes. As the most numerous mammal on the planet, humans are a big part of the mosquito's dinner buffet.

How They Bite

The female uses her sight and her ability to detect the host's heat and carbon dioxide (from exhaling) in order to locate a warm-blooded host. She pierces the host's skin and releases an anticoagulant, a blood thinner of sorts, into the host. Proteins found in the insect's saliva create the itch and welt after the mosquito bites.

How Afraid Should I Be?

Mosquito-borne diseases such as malaria are a serious health threat in much of the world. Thankfully, in the Great Lakes region, mosquito bites are mostly just a painful irritation. Still, several diseases remain a concern.

WEST NILE VIRUS

- Mosquitoes are the main means of contracting **West Nile virus** (WNV), which interferes with the central nervous system and causes inflammation of brain tissue. A mosquito may become infected with the virus by feeding on dead birds; if an infected mosquito bites a human or animal, the virus may be injected into the new host.

- Your risk of becoming seriously ill from **WNV** is very low. Even in areas where the virus is circulating, very few mosquitoes are infected. And fewer than one in 150 people who are bitten and become infected get severely ill. People over 50 years old or chronically ill are at the highest risk of developing severe symptoms.

- Most people infected with **WNV** will not show symptoms. Others might experience mild symptoms such as fever, headache, nausea or vomiting and sometimes swollen lymph glands or a skin rash on the torso. Mild symptoms can last from a few days to several weeks. Severe symptoms include high fever, headache, stupor, coma, vision loss, numbness and paralysis. These symptoms might last for several weeks and the effects could be permanent.

EASTERN EQUINE ENCEPHALITIS

- Of all the viral diseases carried by mosquitoes in the United States, **eastern equine encephalitis** (EEE) is the deadliest to humans. It proves fatal in approximately one-third to one-half of all cases. Survivors often suffer mild to severe permanent neurological damage.

- On the positive side, you are statistically more likely to drown than get mosquito-borne **EEE**. In the past 40 years there have been less than six cases per year.

- **EEE** shows up roughly three days after being bitten by an infected mosquito. Many people infected with **EEE** have no signs of the illness. For those that develop the disease the symptoms are generally like a mild flu. Others develop an inflammation of the brain, lapse into a coma and die.

Preventing Mosquito Bites

PHYSICAL BARRIERS

The most effective means of dealing with mosquitoes is to put a barrier between yourself and the insect.

- Limit your time outdoors at dusk and dawn, when mosquitoes are most active.

- Wear loose-fitting, light-colored clothes that allow air movement but prevent the probing of mosquitoes. Dark clothing attracts mosquitoes.

- Head nets and bug jackets made of fine mesh keep insects from reaching your skin, yet allow air movement. Some are made to absorb repellents.

- Use screen tents to enclose picnic tables and lawn chairs.

NATURAL MOSQUITO REPELLENTS

- Oil of lemon eucalyptus repels mosquitoes. Citronella can work, too, but must be applied more often than synthetic chemicals. Some claim success using Avon Skin So Soft. Others believe eating one clove of raw garlic each day will give their skin an odor that keeps mosquitoes at bay.

- Outdoor products such as mosquito coils and citronella candles or torches can create an uncomfortable air space for mosquitoes.

CHEMICAL REPELLENTS

- The most common and effective repellent ingredient is DEET (di-ethyl-tolumide). However, it can cause eye and sinus irritation, headaches, insomnia and confusion. Repellants with high DEET concentrations can melt nylon, dissolve paint and leave unappealing odors.

- Permethrin is a synthetic, broad-spectrum insecticide. It is ineffective on your skin, yet very durable on clothing and gear.

THINK TWICE

Synthetic repellents and insecticides are dangerous chemicals potentially harmful to you and the environment. Apply them with care, and always read and follow the label instructions.

OTHER TRICKS IN OUTWITTING MOSQUITOES

- When setting up your camp or picnic, choose a location with good air flow, away from thick underbrush and low areas.

- Learn to put up with them! Your body is amazingly adaptable and you will build up a natural resistance over time.

Treatment of Bites

- Soak a washcloth with cool water and press it on the bite.

- Products such as Benadryl and other anti-itch and anti-inflammatory medicines help relieve itching and swelling.

- The juice from a piece of aloe vera plant can be rubbed on bites for relief.

- Apply a simple paste made of baking soda and water (use only enough water to form a sticky paste).

- Jewelweed or touch-me-not (*Impatiens biflora*) can help reduce itching. Pull up a plant from a site where it is abundant, squeeze its succulent stem and roots until it is juicy and rub the plant juices on the affected area.

BOTTOM LINE

Mosquitoes are one of the most abundant "biters" you may encounter outdoors. Fortunately, they are mostly just a painful irritation. Though several mosquito-borne diseases occur in the Great Lakes area, your chances of being infected are remote.

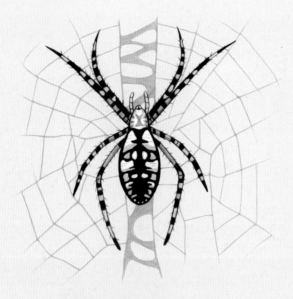

Spiders

In E. B. White's classic tale *Charlotte's Web*, we are introduced to a sweet spider heroine, Charlotte. Even her charming manner and good web penmanship could not lift spiders out of their reputation of permanent Halloween status. Humans have maligned these amazing architects for eons.

Take a close look at a spider and it will mesmerize you with the engineering of its beautiful webs, its patience, stealth and sheer beauty. Who could resist the loving stare of eight eyes?

About Spiders

There are currently more than 35,000 known species of spiders with thousands of additional species waiting to be classified. The U.S. is home to roughly 3,500 spider species, and approximately 1,000 reside in the Great Lakes region.

Life and Times . . .

Spiders, like insects, are invertebrates (without a backbone). Unlike insects they have eight legs and two primary body parts: the cephalothorax (front body section) and the larger abdomen. Like their tick, mite and scorpion cousins, spiders are arachnids.

All species of spiders create silk and all are hunters. They either actively hunt or they hunt from a web.

There are many functions of spider silk. It is used in web-building, egg cases, for wrapping up prey and as a material for creating retreat shelters.

Male spiders are smaller than females and a male can often be recognized by his unique pair of pedipalps or "palps." The palps resemble a pair of legs but more accurately resemble a pair of "feelers." They are located directly in front of the pair of legs closest to the spider's face. The tips of the male's palps are swollen, resembling a pair of boxing gloves. These serve as sperm receptacles for mating.

In some species, the male locates the female through the use of pheromones. These are chemicals produced in their bodies to affect the behavior or physiology of others of their species. Among some species, males recognize the silk draglines of a female.

After a cautious courtship, mating will occur. If the male's timing is off, the female might eat him!

Among most species, females generally lay their eggs in the summer, a week or so after mating. The eggs hatch at the same time and some believe that the hundreds of young are born blind. After a few days at the egg, they can see and move. For several days they live off an internal egg yolk. As they mature they learn that their brothers and sisters are quite a tasty food. Cannibalism is not uncommon among young spiders.

At each stage of growth, spiders shed or molt their skin. Once they reach adulthood they no longer molt.

Fascinating Facts

- Spider silk is the strongest of all natural fibers. It compares favorably with steel and is twice as strong as Kevlar of the same weight.

- Baby spiders (spiderlings) often disperse by jumping from an elevated position, emitting strands of silk and letting the wind carry them away. Some adult spiders will also disperse by catching a ride on the wind. This method of moving is referred to as "ballooning." Ballooning is most commonly observed in autumn.

Thanks to Spiders

- When spiders are found in good numbers, sometimes thousands or millions per acre, they can help control insects that cause damage to agricultural crops.

- Some cultures, like the Piaroa Indians in South America, actually eat large spiders and consider them a delicacy.

- Spider venom has been used in designing new drugs for health care.

Myth Busters

MYTH: A spider bit me last night while I was asleep. It couldn't have been anything else.

This is a widespread superstition. It is highly unusual for a spider to come into your bed. (Unless you sleep on the basement or garage floor!) In the unlikely event that a spider gets into your bed, they will not seek you out to bite you. If you happen to roll onto one, it might bite, but it's not likely.

According to some emergency room personnel, unexplained swelling or skin irritation is often blamed on a "spider bite." Nevertheless, when the patient is asked if they actually saw a spider, they almost always say no. Research has shown that over 80% of suspected "spider bites" are caused by other insects, ticks or by medical conditions.

Why They Bite

The primary reason a spider bites is to kill its prey, and almost all species of spiders are venomous. The venom helps them quickly kill or paralyze their prey.

When a spider bites a human, it is not interested in wrapping you in silk, it is strictly a defensive act. Around humans spiders are generally very timid and will skitter away quickly if they are disturbed.

THINK TWICE

Think twice before calling a daddy longlegs a spider. They are non-venomous arachnids that belong to a group called harvestmen.

Think twice about stepping on a spider caught indoors. By carefully catching and releasing the spider outside, you will model caring behavior to your children and others.

Around the world there is a universal belief that it is unlucky to kill a spider. In fact there is a popular old English rhyme that speaks to such compassion towards spiders: "If you wish to live and thrive let a spider run alive."

How They Bite

Actually, spiders don't bite, they inject. The spider's mouth is located directly below their eyes. Their large jaws are called chelicerae and these vertical structures are often lined with small teeth and tipped with fangs. In most spiders, these jaws swing inward from the sides to grasp prey. In some larger spider species, the jaws swing downwards to more easily pin down their prey.

The spider's venom is secreted through two fangs into their prey, but spiders less than about ⁵/₁₆ of an inch cannot bite you, as they are too small. Pretty much all spiders larger than ⁵/₁₆ of an inch can bite humans, but most usually *won't*. Even those which can break your skin will sometimes inject harmless venom, and some will not inject venom at all. Most spider bites are less painful than a bee sting, but some people are more sensitive to spider bites than others.

How Afraid Should I Be?

In the Great Lakes region, the majority of species of spiders are harmless. Having said that, there are very rare cases where people might be sensitive to a bite. Larry Weber, author of *Spiders of the North Woods,* told me that in over 30 years of collecting and studying spiders, only two spiders have broken his skin with their bites and both resulted in only a temporary itch. (And one of those was in South Carolina!)

The only two species that are cause for concern in this region are the brown recluse spider and the black widow spider. Neither of these species is common to this region, as they prefer more southerly latitudes.

brown recluse

The brown recluse spider is colored tan to dark brown and is approximately ¹/₂ of an inch long. It bears a distinctive dark violin-shaped marking on top of the front body section (cephalothorax).

Its bite is usually painless but a burning sensation is commonly experienced in the first hour. After several hours, a blister forms and the surrounding skin begins to darken and swell. The venom of the brown recluse might cause extensive tissue damage. It normally takes up to two months for such a bite to heal.

The black widow is a very shy species. The female delivers a serious, but rarely lethal, bite. (The male is too small to bite humans.) The female has a round, shiny black abdomen with a red, hourglass-shaped marking on the underside of her belly.

Her bite might feel like a pinprick. The bite site

black widow

might swell lightly and bear faint red marks. Within a few hours, the pain intensifies and stiffness begins. Other symptoms of the neurotoxic venom include chills, fever, nausea and severe abdominal pain.

Keep in mind, confirmed bites from black widow and brown recluse spiders are *extremely* rare in the Great Lakes region.

Preventing Spider Bites

- Avoid handling spiders with your bare hands. When removing spiders from your home, gently cover them with a glass or jar, slide a piece of paper underneath and release them outdoors.
- Don't reach into dusty, dark recesses with your bare hands.

Treatment of Bites

- Clean and wash the bite site with soap and hot water.
- Apply ice and elevate the affected area.
- To guard against infection, apply an antiseptic lotion or cream.
- Most bites improve within a few hours to three days.
- Seek medical attention if symptoms persist or worsen. This is especially important with children.
- In the highly unlikely event that a brown recluse or black widow bites you, capture the spider for positive identification and seek immediate medical attention.

BOTTOM LINE

Spiders are timid around people and skitter away if disturbed. If one does bite you, it is strictly in self-defense. In the Great Lakes region, nearly all spider bites are harmless to humans and less painful than a bee sting.

Deer and Horse Flies

Every summer, I shudder when I hear the simple declaration, "The deer flies are out." Along with horse flies, these persistent biters can turn an otherwise perfect day at the beach, garden or in the boat into a sore test of endurance.

Sometimes, though, they help us see the larger drama of life. I recall one day in my garden. As I crawled down a row of peas, deer flies flew laps around my head and occasionally stole in for a quick bite. Suddenly I heard a clattering of wings overhead. I tipped my head to sneak a peek. A dragonfly! Soon a second joined it. I heard more clattering and even felt light taps on my hat. They were picking off deer flies that alighted on my head! In a sense, I had become a dragonfly feeder. By attracting the deer flies I provided easy pickings for the predators. What had been a pest to me was sustenance for the dragonflies.

About Deer and Horse Flies

This is a well-represented group of flies. There are approximately 4,300 species in the world, with more than 160 species of horse flies and over 110 types of deer flies occurring in the continental United States. Both deer and horse flies have similar life cycles.

deer fly

horse fly

Deer flies are the smaller of the two. They measure about $\frac{1}{4}$- to $\frac{3}{8}$-inch long. They are commonly tan-colored with distinct dark patches on their wings. Their antennae are slightly longer than their heads. They are strong fliers and are usually not solitary.

The larger horse fly averages $\frac{1}{2}$- to $1\frac{1}{4}$-inch long and is more robust. Its wings have no patches and are uniformly cloudy. Antennae are shorter than the head and thick at the base. Horse fly eyes are large and appear colorful.

Both flies are dependent on wetlands such as marshes, ponds or slow-moving streams to complete their life cycles. As adults, they can cover wide areas. Deer flies are particularly fond of brush, woods and meadows. Horse flies tend to be more common around larger bodies of water like lakes.

Life and Times . . .

In the Great Lakes region, deer flies typically make their appearance in June and stay with us into August. Prior to mating, both males and females feed on plant nectars and juices. After mating, the female seeks a meal of blood.

Males are rarely seen but can be distinguished from females by their large compound eyes, which touch each other; the female's eyes are distinctly separated.

deer fly laying eggs

The female will lay a single mass of 100–800 eggs on the underside of a leaf or on the stem of a plant growing out of a wetland. Freshly laid egg masses are whitish and soon darken upon exposure to air.

In 2–3 days, the eggs hatch and the larvae drop down into the water or mud to complete their development. The last larval stage spends the winter dormant in the wetland. The following spring, the larvae shed their skin and proceed to the pupal stage. It takes 1–3 weeks for the adult fly to pupate. Most deer and horse flies pupate on the edge of marshes, swamps and ponds.

The larvae of deer flies feed on insects and plant material. On the other hand, all studied species of horse fly larvae eat other insects.

Fascinating Facts

- Only female deer and horse flies bite.
- The mating flight for these flies is generally in the early morning. Only after this does the female require a blood meal.
- Some of the larger species of horse flies require 2–3 years of development in an aquatic environment before they emerge as adults.

Thanks to Deer Flies and Horse Flies

- Both of these flies are important prey species for many birds and other insects.

- The aquatic larvae of deer and horse flies provide a food source for many species of fish.

- The males of each species are important plant pollinators.

Myth Busters

MYTH: Swatting at deer flies will chase them away.

It won't. In fact, the motion will agitate them and probably attract more.

Why They Bite

With some exceptions, the female deer or horse fly needs to feed on blood in order to produce viable eggs. Like all other biting flies, they only bite during daylight hours—lying in ambush in the shade of brush or trees and swarming around any passing potential host. They zero in on a target by noting movement, the release of carbon dioxide (emitted when you exhale) and odors such as fragrant perfumes or shampoos.

How They Bite

Deer and horse fly bites are painfully similar. A tiny pair of blade-like mandibles lacerates the skin, causing blood flow—which is lapped up with a sponge-like mouthpart. Like mosquitoes, these flies incorporate an anticoagulant into the bite to make the wound bleed more freely. A bite often results in a small red welt that might persist for several days. Slight swelling and itchiness may occur at the site of the bite.

If deer or horse flies are numerous enough they will change your outdoor

horse fly

plans. Of the two species of flies, I consider the deer fly a greater pest. Some folks claim, "A deer fly is a black fly on steroids!"

How Afraid Should I Be?

Deer and horse fly bites are generally not serious injuries. But they can result in open wounds and a possible secondary infection. Aggressively scratching the affected area can make matters worse.

Even if deer flies only occasionally bite you, they are extremely annoying as they swirl in a horde around your head. Ironically, they seem to flock to moving targets. In other words if you restrict your movements you will be less of a target. Luckily, neither the horse nor deer fly will enter your tent or home to seek you out. If you have ever noticed a wayward deer or horse fly in a house or vehicle, they are usually bouncing off a window trying to get out.

Preventing Deer and Horse Fly Bites

- The best prevention for keeping both of these biting flies at bay is to cover up. When deer fly season is underway, I don't leave home without a hat.

- Repellents do not work.

- Avoid deer and horse fly habitat during midsummer.

- Some outdoor workers and enthusiasts have good success with deer fly "patches." Non-toxic and odorless, the double-sided adhesive patches work like portable fly strips. Press one to the back of your hat or cap and it will attract circling deer flies—which find themselves stuck upon landing.

- Deer flies typically go after the tallest person in a group, as well as the one walking in front. Use this tip wisely. If the hike leader turns to you complaining about the deer flies, swing your hands wildly at imaginary antagonists and grumble loudly!

- I have had some success sticking the stems of tall bracken ferns down the back of my shirt, so the front projects like an umbrella above my head. This creates a canopy of ferns over my head that does a decent job of distracting the deer flies. I think it looks cool, too.

- I have a neighbor who swears that affixing a blue—yes blue—Dixie cup to the top of her head attracts deer flies to the cup instead of her head. (I'll stick to ferns, myself.)

Treatment of Bites

Wash bites with warm water and soap. Benadryl and other anti-itch or anti-inflammatory compounds, lotions and creams can provide itching relief.

BOTTOM LINE

Deer and horse fly bites are slightly painful but generally not dangerous. The bite may produce a small, red welt accompanied by minor swelling and itching that lasts several days. Wearing a hat, long-sleeved shirt and long pants can help prevent most bites.

Hornets, Wasps and Yellowjackets

No group of insects urges humans to retreat faster than wasps, hornets, yellowjackets and bees. They wear their stripes well. We have come to learn that the distinct pattern of belted stripes encircling the bodies of this fierce crew is a clear visual warning to "Watch Out!" While most encounters are benign, their stings are painful and, for some people, allergic reactions to the venom can be life-threatening.

About Hornets, Wasps and Yellowjackets

Like honey bees and bumblebees, these thin-waisted stingers live in social colonies made up of workers (infertile females), queens and males. Hornets, wasps and yellowjackets in particular are more aggressive than honey bees.

yellowjacket

wasp

hornet

Life and Times . . .

Colonies of hornets, wasps and yellowjackets remain active for only one summer, after which the fertilized queens fly away to start more colonies. Other colony members die at the end of the summer and the nest is not reused.

Fertilized queens winter in protected places such as hollow logs, stumps, under bark, in leaf litter, abandoned animal dens and manmade structures. They emerge in the warm days of late April and early May to select a nest site and build a small paper nest in which to lay their eggs.

After her first brood hatches, a queen feeds the young larvae for about 18–20 days. These young will eventually pupate and emerge around mid-June as the colony's first group of workers. Infertile females, their jobs will include foraging for food, defending the nest, and caring for the queen's subsequent hatches of larvae. Each cell in the nest may be used for two or three batches of broods.

The larvae's primary diet are protein-rich foods such as insects, meats and fish. Adults are particularly fond of fruits, flower nectar and tree sap, which provide ample doses of sugars and carbohydrates.

The queen stays with her nest throughout the summer, laying eggs. Eventually she might build an empire of several thousand workers. In late August and early September, she creates cells where future queens and males are produced. They are cared for and fed by the sterile workers before leaving the colony in the fall for a mating flight. After mating, the males die and fertilized queens look for protected sites to spend the winter.

BALD-FACED HORNET IDENTIFICATION

The bald-faced hornet is similar to a paper wasp and yellowjacket. Two primary differences involve the hornet's nest and physical appearance.

bald-faced hornet nest

- The bald-faced hornet's nest is ball- or oval-shaped and can be larger than a basketball. Nests are most often constructed on a tree limb or shrub branch. Hidden by summer foliage, they are most easily viewed after the leaves fall in autumn.

- The hornet itself is large, black and thin-waisted. It is named for its distinctive white or "bald" face.

PAPER WASP IDENTIFICATION

The queen paper wasp creates a single layer of cells that is attached by a "stem" to the underside of eaves, benches and other protected overhangs.

Paper wasps, like yellowjackets, are striped in yellow and black. However they are slightly larger (particularly in the abdomen) than yellowjackets.

paper wasp nest

YELLOWJACKET IDENTIFICATION

Of the three groups, yellowjackets are the only one that often nests underground. Sometimes they nest behind the siding of a building or in a building crevice.

yellowjacket underground nest

Fascinating Facts

- Wasps and hornets make their papery nests by chewing on tiny pieces of wood, bark or even cardboard. They add their saliva to the chewed wood and "paint" it into a smooth, thin material used for making the nest. The various colors of the rather artful nest are determined by the source of the wood.

- Of the approximately 15,000 species of stinging wasps in the world, 95% of them do not sting humans.

- After the nests freeze in the fall, any remaining larvae are dead. These frozen treats are high in fat and are desirable food items for squirrels, skunks and even birds such as woodpeckers and blue jays.

- The stinger on this group of insects has evolved from the long, sharp portion of the insect called the ovipositor. It is also the mechanism from which eggs are deposited.

Thanks to Hornets, Wasps and Yellowjackets

- Worker wasps and hornets feed on caterpillars and other insects that are often harmful to human food crops. These include corn earworms, armyworms, tobacco hornworms, house flies, blowflies and other harmful caterpillars.

- Although they lack the pollen-carrying structures of bees, yellowjackets can be minor pollinators when visiting flowers.

- They often eat the flesh of dead animals, making them important members of the "cleanup crew."

Myth Busters

MYTH: All bees and wasps sting.

Many wasps are non-stinging and most do not sting humans. Only female wasps are capable of inflicting a sting. Males are rarely seen since their function is to mate during the fall mating flight.

And just because a wasp or a hornet looks scary doesn't mean it will sting you. The ichneumon wasp has a long ovipositor (a tube for depositing eggs) at the end of its body, and this tube is spooky-looking and looks like a stinger. But it's not. The wasp drills the ovipositor into soft or rotting wood and lays its eggs.

Myth: Just because an insect looks like a wasp or hornet, it is one.

Actually, many harmless insects look a lot like wasps or hornets. Many insect species mimic the colors of their feistier neighbors in order to protect themselves. If an insect looks like a yellowjacket, wasp, or hornet, birds and other predators think twice before attacking, as the predators see the bright colors and sometimes shy away. But many innocent insects are often confused for wasps or hornets and unfairly swatted. Just because an insect looks like a wasp or a hornet, it doesn't mean it is one.

Why They Sting

The primary function of the sting in this group of insects is to kill prey. They are predators. Secondly, they use the sting to defend themselves or the colony. They simply do not seek out humans to randomly sting. While your intentions might be totally innocent, if the hornet, wasp or yellowjacket perceives you as a threat, it will sting you.

bald-faced hornet

How They Sting

The stinger is located in the tip of the abdomen. Unlike honey bees—which can only sting once—hornets, wasps and yellowjackets do not lose their stinger and can sting repeatedly. The dose of toxin is less than that of a honey bee and is lessened with each sting. When a hornet, wasp or yellowjacket stings, the two halves of the abdomen casing open up to allow the stinger to emerge. The stinger is made up of a piercing stylet and two tiny, flanking lancets.

The sting happens when the stinger is thrust into the victim and the micro-lancets move back and forth like a saw. These lancets are slightly barbed at the edges. Anchored in the flesh, the moving lancets trigger a pumping action at the end of the abdomen, causing the poison sac to pump venom into the wound. Since hornets, wasps and yellowjackets have smaller barbs on their lancets than a honey bee, they can pull the shaft out and fly happily away. On the other hand, the honey bee's stinger stays fixed in the flesh and when it pulls away, it literally pulls out the stinger and venom sac. The injury results in the bee's death.

The sting of hornets contains acetylcholine, which stimulates pain nerves more than the stings of other wasps and bees. So they can be a bit more painful.

How Afraid Should I Be?

There is no need to fear these insects. Respect, yes, but not fear. Most of their lives are spent trying to make a living, searching for food for themselves and the brood. Any attack on you is time spent away from foraging.

Minimize attacks through avoidance, staying calm and being alert. For example, in late summer foraging yellowjackets become a nuisance when they change from eating meat to a diet of ripe, rotting fruit, human garbage, sweet drinks and picnic foods. By understanding their behavior and responding accordingly, we can prevent most attacks.

Preventing Stings

- Hornets, wasps and particularly yellowjackets are very defensive around their nests. If you locate nests, simply note them and avoid them, telling other people

THINK TWICE

I often let these uninvited guests to the picnic have a few bites of my sandwich or dessert and then move on. Another trick is to simply place a dab of food on a napkin and set it in the middle of the table as a decoy to attract these insects. It also makes for an interesting and educational centerpiece Don't worry about insect germs, you receive far more when you hug or shake hands with human guests at the picnic.

Think twice about trying to kill a hornet, wasp or yellowjacket that you discover while driving your car. Slowly pull over to the side of the road and open the windows and doors so it can fly out. You are in far more danger of initiating a car accident if you try to get the insect out while you're behind the wheel.

who frequent the area. I would not recommend nest eradication unless the nest poses a threat to humans. I have had very good success in preventing wasp nest construction by applying a thin film of petroleum jelly underneath picnic tabletops and seats, deck benches etc. If you must get rid of a nest, plan to remove it early in the morning or later in the evening, when cooler temperatures have ushered the inhabitants into the nest. If you are using a chemical, read and carefully follow the label directions.

wasp

- Avoiding fragrant soaps, shampoos, perfumes, after-shaves and colognes. Hornets, wasps and yellowjackets are sometimes attracted to them.

- Keep children from throwing rocks at nests or spraying them with water. Avoid making loud noises or disturbing the nests.

- Some folks have luck with yellowjacket/hornet traps that are placed outside a home or near a picnic site. The sweet bait lures them into the trap, from which there is no exit.

Treatment of Stings

- Wash the site of the sting with soap and water, and apply ice to minimize swelling and pain. Mixing a solution of ½ of a teaspoon meat tenderizer with a teaspoon of water and placing it on the wound can minimize discomfort.

- Pay close attention to how you feel after a sting. Allergic reactions to the venom occur in approximately 1% of the human population. If someone else is stung, watch them for about an hour. Seek immediate medical attention if you notice any change in breathing, scratchiness in the throat or symptoms of hives. In the meantime, keep the victim quiet, calm and as still as possible.

- If you know that you or one of your family members is allergic to bee or wasp venom ask your doctor for a prescription for either an Anaphylaxis Emergency Treatment Kit or an EpiPen. Both contain injectable adrenaline (epinephrine) for allergic reactions. Carry your kit or EpiPen with you at all times during the peak hornet, wasp and yellowjacket season. Carefully follow instructions to administer the epinephrine.

BOTTOM LINE

Hornets, wasps and yellowjackets deserve respect, not fear. Most of their lives are spent trying to find food for themselves and their broods. Stings are purely defensive attacks that can be minimized through avoidance, staying calm and being alert.

Honey Bees

The honey bee is arguably the most valuable insect to our well-being. Not only do they provide us with a wonderful sweetener but they also add approximately $15 billion in value to agricultural crops such as apples, almonds, berries, other fruits and vegetables.

On the downside, the honey bee is likely responsible for more human deaths and near-death experiences than any other wild creature in the Great Lakes region. Every year approximately 50 people die in the United States from allergic reactions to bee and wasp stings.

About Honey Bees

Seven species of honey bees produce and store honey and build colonial nests out of wax produced by the colony workers. The western honey bee is the subspecies that has been domesticated for honey and wax production. Not native to North America, honey bees were introduced from Europe nearly 400 years ago by early colonists.

Life and Times . . .

Generally, most of the bees in a colony or hive all have the same mother; she is known as the queen bee. There is one queen per colony. She makes one or two mating flights in her life. After mating with one or several males (drones) she is able to store millions of sperm cells in her body. She is capable of living for several years and during that period she will lay tens of thousands of eggs.

Most of the bees in the colony are non-fertile females. These worker bees live only 6 weeks in the summer and 4–9 months during the winter months. They are highly organized and assume many roles. Some are nurse bees, others forage for nectar and pollen, others guard the colony, some work on constructing the hive and others tend the queen as her royal attendants. While we might think it is grim, the chore of cleaning dead bees out of the hive is simply a natural task for another group of bees.

The bumblebee has a similar life cycle. Like honey bees, they also produce honey and live in colonies. If you see a large bumblebee buzzing loudly among spring's first flowers, it is likely a queen bee gathering pollen for her underground nest.

honey bee hive

Of the entire hive, only the fertilized queen survives the winter. She lays her eggs on the pollen and covers them with wax. After 4–5 days the eggs hatch and the larvae feed on the stored pollen. The larvae pupate into cocoons and after nearly two weeks, the queen strips off the wax and the bees emerge. These are infertile workers.

Later in the summer the queen lays eggs that produce males and fertile females. They will leave the nest and mate. Only queens that have successfully mated will overwinter. All others, including the summer queen, will die.

Fascinating Facts

- Even separated from the bee, the venom sac continues to pump venom into the skin for approximately two minutes.

- Only the female honey bee is equipped with the slightly barbed stinger.

- A bumblebee's loud buzzing is not caused by its wings, but rather the bee vibrating its flight muscles. Bumblebees and honey bees can do this when the muscles are purposely disengaged from the wings.

- Due to the bumblebee's large size, it must warm up before flying in chilly weather.

- Bees have two stomachs. One is for storing gathered flower nectar and the other is their regular stomach. When full, the nectar-bearing stomach weighs almost as much as the bee does. Bees must visit 100 to 1,500 flowers in order to "fill up" on nectar.

Thanks to Honey Bees

- Some plants need honey bee pollination as much as they need water and sunlight. The U.S. Department of Agriculture estimates that $1/3$ of our daily diet relies on insect pollination, of which honey bees perform a full 80%.

- Bee venom contains a very potent anti-inflammatory agent and is used by many people in managing joint pain, arthritis and even multiple sclerosis.

- Bees pollinate many types of trees that cause allergy problems for some folks. Honey produced from the pollen of these trees' flowers helps minimize the misery.

- Beekeeping is a vital occupation for thousands of people. Products include honey, pollen and beeswax.

Myth Busters

MYTH: A honey bee can sting you over and over.

When the bee pulls away after stinging you, it pulls away a portion of its abdomen, resulting in the bee's death. She is willing to give up her life to defend herself or the hive.

Why They Sting

Bees sting for two primary reasons: to defend themselves and to defend their colony. Like wasps, hornets and yellowjackets, bees do not go out looking for victims to sting.

How They Sting

A bee's stinger is a formidable weapon. It consists of two sharp, curved blades with 8–10 barbs near the tip. A narrow duct is formed when the two blades are positioned next to each other. This duct serves as the channel in which the venom is delivered from the venom sac. Muscles at the stinger force the barb into the flesh and then muscles pump the venom into the flesh.

THINK TWICE

Think twice before you investigate a bee hive without supervision from a beekeeper and the protection of proper beekeeping clothing.

Think twice before picking a lovely bouquet of flowers. Carefully inspect the blossoms so as not to disturb a foraging bee.

When you are stung, the stinger emits a pheromonal alarm (a mixture of chemical compounds designed to provoke a certain behavior), smelled by other bees, that quickly warns them to maintain alertness and get ready to attack.

How Afraid Should I Be?

Given that honey bees and bumblebees are not normally aggressive and are far more interested in working for the welfare of the home hive, they are not usually a problem. However, if you know or suspect you are allergic to bee venom, be proactive and seek a doctor who will prescribe the proper medication. Then it is up to you to have it accessible when outdoors.

Most human deaths occur in the first hour after getting stung.

Preventing Bee Stings

- If a bee is flying around you, simply ignore it or gently urge it away.

- Flailing your arms and swinging at it might provoke defensive behavior and that could result in a sting.

- Avoid strong-scented skin products, soaps and shampoos.

- If you are working in a flower garden or find yourself anywhere that bees gather perhaps the best preparation is to simply wear proper clothing that minimizes skin exposure. Mosquito repellents are ineffective against bees.

- Bees sometimes swarm in the most unusual places. Officials at a major league baseball game once had to call a timeout while a beekeeper removed a swarm that had clustered in one of the dugouts!

honey bee covered with pollen

- Swarmed bees are rarely aggressive and you should be patient and let them move on their way. Sometimes the swarm can linger for a couple of days. Please do NOT kill them with a pesticide. At the very least contact a local beekeeper and they will be happy to remove the bees to create a new hive for their beekeeping yard.

Treatment of Stings

- Immediately remove the stinger and venom sac by carefully scraping the stinger with a fingernail or knife blade. DO NOT grasp the stinger with your fingers or a tweezers or you will only force venom into the wound.

- You can also purchase an extractor to remove the venom from the site of the sting. However, the usual sting does not happen within two minutes of a first aid kit—the likely place to keep a venom extractor.

- Wash the site of the sting with soap and water and apply ice to minimize swelling and pain. Mixing a solution of ½ of a teaspoon meat tenderizer and a teaspoon of water and placing it on the wound can minimize discomfort.

- Pay close attention to how you feel after a sting. Allergic reactions to the bee's venom occur in approximately 1% of the human population. If someone else is stung, watch them closely and seek immediate medical attention if you notice any change in breathing, scratchiness in the throat or symptoms of hives. In the meantime, keep the victim quiet, calm and as still as possible.

- If you or one of your family members is allergic to bee stings, ask your doctor for a prescription for either an Anaphylaxis Emergency Treatment Kit or an EpiPen. Both contain injectable adrenaline (epinephrine) for allergic reactions. Carry your kit or EpiPen with you at all times during the peak bee season. Carefully follow instructions to administer the epinephrine.

BOTTOM LINE

There is no reason to fear honey bees and bumblebees. They only sting to defend themselves or their colony. When a bee buzzes around you, enjoy the unique "music" of this beneficial little insect, or gently urge it away. Flailing your arms might provoke defensive behavior—and a sting.

Giant Water Bugs

There are approximately one hundred species of giant water bugs in the world. Though fierce-looking, they are often prepared as a human food item in parts of Asia and elsewhere. At the Typhoon Restaurant in Santa Monica, California, you can get a pair of chicken-stuffed water bugs, deep-fried and seasoned Thai style, for $8!

About Giant Water Bugs

Its name sounds like something out of a science fiction movie, and indeed the giant water bug is an oversize, nasty-looking insect. Also known as a "Toe Biter" or "Fish Killer," it can grow to about two inches in length.

Humans most often see giant water bugs on land but they spend most of their lives in the water—where your chances of a bite are greatest. While a bite from this insect can be painful, it is highly unlikely to happen. This sinister-looking bug avoids human contact whenever possible.

Life and Times . . .

Giant water bugs (*Lethocerus sp.*) are the Goliaths of Great Lakes insects. As their name suggests, they live in water, preferring still or slow-flowing areas with an abundance of vegetation. Voracious predators, they hunt by ambush from their hideouts in aquatic plants or dead leaves on the bottom of the wetland.

They grasp other insects, tadpoles, small fish and salamanders with their large, strong front legs, then inject venom produced from their salivary glands. These toxins paralyze the prey and liquefy its insides—which are then sucked up through the giant water bug's straw-like beak.

The male of some giant water bug species carries hundreds of eggs on its back. The female fastens them there with a glue-like substance and the male fans water over them with his legs. The behavior, called back brooding, reduces the risk of having the eggs dry up, keeps water flowing over the eggs and protects them from predators.

Despite their size, giant water bugs are hard to spot unless you're looking for them. Although you may catch a glimpse of one recharging its air supply at the surface, they spend much of their time on the bottom or hiding among the leaves and stalks of aquatic plants.

Fascinating Facts

- Giant water bugs often take wing at night in search of a new home or mate. But such flights are risky: Entomologists believe artificial lights confuse the insects, causing them to fly around the lights until they die.

- Adults breathe air at the surface using two short tubes located at the tip of the abdomen. The air is stored in a bubble under the wings, where it supplies oxygen during dives.

- Giant water bugs belong to a rather notorious family tree. They are related to assassin bugs, boxelder bugs and stink bugs.

Thanks to Giant Water Bugs

- These large insects provide food for other predators such as herons, egrets, raccoons, mink and a variety of fish species.

- Giant water bugs also help keep populations of invertebrates in check.

Myth Busters

MYTH: They look scary, so they must be mean.

Yes, giant water bugs look nasty. And they will bite when captured, cornered or otherwise harassed. But they don't go looking for trouble; in fact, they prefer to retreat, hide or even play dead when threatened.

Why They Bite

Unlike mosquitoes and deer flies, giant water bugs don't hunt humans. So unless you resemble a minnow or tadpole, you'll most likely be bitten because you're a threat.

How They Bite

The giant water bug pierces its prey (as well as wayward toes or fingers) with its sharp mouthpart. Toxin is injected into the flesh by a needle-like beak. It may also pinch with its powerful front legs.

How Afraid Should I Be?

Unless you actively seek out and handle giant water bugs, your chances of being bitten are low. The odds drop even more if you avoid areas with aquatic vegetation, and fall to near zero if you stay out of the water.

If you are bitten, grit your teeth. The injected toxin causes what is reportedly the most painful of all insect bites. It is often accompanied by inflammation below the bite. Most people quickly recover with no lasting ill-effects. However, because there is venom in the bite, there is the possibility of an anaphylactic reaction.

Preventing Giant Water Bug Bites

Since this beefy bug hides out in weeds in still or slow-moving water, the best way to avoid it is stay out of the water—particularly weedy areas.

THINK TWICE

Think twice if you're tempted to pick up a giant water bug for a closer look—you're risking a painful bite. If you simply must inspect one, keep your fingers away from its head and mouthparts. And never assume a "dead" bug is safe to handle. It may only be feigning death.

- If you feel compelled to pick one up to inspect it, do so carefully! Firmly hold the insect between your thumb and forefinger, grasping its sides or back and underside—never the head.

- Wearing water shoes or an old pair of tennis shoes while wading will help protect your toes and feet from encounters with giant water bugs.

Treatment of Bites

- If you or anyone in your family is known to have an allergic reaction to stings and bites, you should get a prescription for an EpiPen. The EpiPen is a combined syringe and needle that injects a single dose of medication. Be sure your doctor shows you and other members of your family how to use the EpiPen properly.

- Watch the giant water bug bite site for several days. If the wound becomes discolored and the flesh appears to rot, seek medical assistance.

BOTTOM LINE

Giant water bugs look scary but unless you resemble a tadpole, they're not out to get you. If you don't handle or otherwise harass them, your chances of being bitten are low. The risk factor drops even more if you avoid areas with aquatic plants, and falls off the chart on dry land.

Leeches

"If there is anything in the world I hate, it's leeches. Oh, the filthy little devils!"
—Humphrey Bogart as Charlie in the movie, *The African Queen*

I am haunted by the image of Bogart standing on the deck of the *African Queen* covered in leeches. And yet for over 2,000 years, leeches have played a profound role in treating various human ailments. How is it that these same graceful swimming animals don't inspire applause for their role in medicine?

About Leeches

Leeches are common in the Great Lakes region. Among many species, the adults are large, dark, segmented aquatic worms with a strong, clinging sucker at each end. The front sucker, where the mouth is located, can be very small. Many leeches are strong swimmers as witnessed by their rippling movements through the water. They are commonly found hiding in muck or submerged vegetation in quiet sections of lakes, ponds, marshes and other wetlands.

Life and Times . . .

Leeches are parasites that depend on a host from which to feed on blood. Some feed on the blood of humans and other mammals, while others feed on fish, turtles, frogs or birds. Some leeches even feed on other blood-engorged leeches.

Leeches are unique in that there are no females and no males! They are hermaphrodites. That means they have both male and female sex organs. When they mate, they intertwine their bodies and deposit sperm in the other's clitellum. (This is the raised band where the sex organs are located. It is very obvious in an earthworm.)

After fertilization takes place, the clitellum secretes a tough, jelly-like cocoon that contains nutrients. The eggs are deposited in this mass. The released cocoon is either buried or attached to a stick or rock. After weeks or even months, the young leeches emerge looking like tiny adults. Leeches usually die after one or two reproductive episodes.

Fascinating Facts

- In 2003, a boy in Boston had his ear bitten off by a dog. After the ear was reattached there were problems with blood pooling around the wound site. Finally, the only technique that worked was applying leeches around the wound. Now most large hospitals, including the world-famous Mayo Clinic, use leeches in some medical procedures.

- In the 19th century leeches were used to forecast bad weather. Leeches breathe through their body wall and they position themselves to take advantage of their intake of dissolved oxygen. Leeches kept in a jar will swim close to the surface when there is a fall in atmospheric pressure, which often foretells the arrival of rainy, stormy weather.

- In the 1800s, barbers not only cut hair, they often relieved patients of supposedly "bad" blood with the help of leeches. The familiar red-and-white striped pole found outside a barbershop represented blood and bandages.

Thanks to Leeches

- Many fishes, wading birds such as herons and egrets, and other animals feed on leeches and bloodsuckers.

- The bite of a leech produces a small, bleeding wound that mimics blood flow. Consequently, the leech is becoming more and more valuable for plastic and reconstructive surgery.

Myth Busters

MYTH: Water-resistant insect repellents will keep leeches off you.

There is no evidence of any repellent or home remedy that will effectively discourage leeches from feeding on you. These include coating exposed body parts with bath soap, eucalyptus oil or lemon juice.

Why They Bite

The soft, stealthy bite of a leech is simply to gain access to blood. They do not defend themselves by biting.

How They Bite

After detecting potential prey with the help of sensory organs on the surface of its head and body, the leech "inchworms" slowly toward its quarry and then gently attaches itself. The leech's "mouth" is made up of three jaws. Arranged in a Y-shaped pattern, they work together in a sawing motion. It's a wickedly effective combination, since each jaw can contain about 100 teeth!

The leech's saliva is like a pharmacy, containing an assortment of chemicals that help it feed. There's an anesthetic to minimize the pain. (If a leech can be sneaky about biting, you won't discover it—and a leech needs time to "download" its blood meal.) There is also a blood thinner (anti-coagulant) to maximize blood flow, and a vasodilator that encourages the opening of blood vessels for easier bleeding. To further speed the process, a spreading factor moves these chemicals easily and quickly. Finally, a bacterium in the leech's gut helps it digest the blood—what a marvelous organism.

How Afraid Should I Be?

You need not be very afraid of a leech attaching itself to you. Firstly, it is a rare occurrence since most folks don't typically find themselves wading barefoot in mucky, "leechy" habitat. Secondly, the bite has no venom and is a very superficial wound. There is no evidence that leeches transmit any diseases.

THINK TWICE

Avoid old-school methods of leech removal such as applying salt or stoically yanking the critter loose. Sprinkling salt on a leech attached to your skin might cause more discomfort than the actual bite. Worse, aggressively pulling on a leech could cause it to literally squeeze its stomach contents into the open wound. Gross!

Preventing Leech Bites

- Stay out of mucky wetlands.

- If you wade into likely leech habitat, wear socks, pantyhose or other clothing that make it impossible for the leech to find your skin.

Treatment of Bites

- If the leech is still attached, the best way to remove it is to press your finger on the skin next to the leech's sucker (mouthparts); next, gently but firmly push your finger toward its sucker and use your fingernail to dislodge it.

- Wash the bite with soap and water. Apply a bandage if necessary. Anticoagulants from the leech might cause oozing of blood for several hours.

- Some irritation and itching might occur after the bite. Benadryl and other anti-itching compounds can provide some relief.

BOTTOM LINE

Don't let a fear of leeches keep you out of the water. There's no reason to be afraid. "Attachments" are rare, unless you regularly wade barefoot in mucky, "leechy" habitat. Their bite has no venom and is harmless.

Bats

One of my earliest memories involves a bat. We were at my grandparents' house for Sunday supper. As the adults chatted while busily cleaning up after eating, I walked into the living room, bored for something to do. There on the floor in front of me was a small, round, furry object. I plunked myself next it. Unsure about what it was, I leaned over and blew on it. And in that moment, the serenity of Sunday was lost.

The bat lifted quietly into the air and flew erratically around the living room and dining room. Is it any wonder that I got scared when I heard the shrill screams from the kitchen and watched grown women shield themselves with dishtowels?

Uh-oh, what had I awakened?!

About Bats

Like spiders, bats have been relegated to the halls of outcasts by virtue of the fact that they are symbols of Halloween as Santa Claus is of Christmas.

Bats are the only true flying mammals. Flying squirrels can take to the air, but depend on gravity and the flap of skin that connects their legs to allow them to glide, not fly.

While there are approximately 950 species of bats in the world, only nine species are found in the Great Lakes region. They are the little brown (most common), big brown, silver-haired, hoary, red, eastern pipistrelle, northern long-eared, evening and Indiana bat.

Life and Times . . .

All bats in this region live on a diet of insects. Consequently, they practice hibernation or migration to cope with cold winters. A hibernating bat survives winter by slowly burning stored fat. By the time spring arrives it is not unusual for them to lose $1/3$ of their body weight.

hoary bat

Even though these bats typically mate in the fall, prior to hibernation or migration, they practice a strategy called "delayed fertilization." Sperm from the male is stored in the female's uterus for up to seven months. Soon after leaving hibernation, the female bat ovulates (releases an egg from her ovary) and the waiting sperm fertilize the egg. Mating requires time and energy, and the practice of delayed fertilization helps bats conserve energy in the early spring, when insects are scarce.

Most bats have one offspring (called a "pup") but some have 2–4. Young bats develop quickly and are flying within three weeks. Bats often congregate in colonies where the females nurse their young. By July and August, the young are flying and hunting insects.

Fascinating Facts

- One out of every five mammal species in the world is a bat!

- As a bat flies in the night sky hunting for insects, it depends on echolocation to locate prey. The bat emits a pulse of very high-pitched squeaks, which are picked up by its oversized ears and used to determine size and location of the prey.

- The echo does not travel far in air, so the bat can only make adjustments when it is within a few yards, hence the reason for its erratic flight.

Thanks to Bats

- Bats are prolific insect eaters capable of devouring 600–1,000 mosquitoes an hour!! Many of the bugs they eat are pests to humans.

- Bats in southern regions are important pollinators of plants, including some that are important for human agriculture.

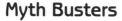

- The discovery of the principle of echolocation in bats helped lead to the development of sonar and radar. We have used the bat as a model to help planes and boats navigate and fishermen locate fish.

Myth Busters

MYTH: Bats are vicious carriers of rabies.

While some bats do transmit rabies, the incidents are very few.

MYTH: If you're not careful, a bat could get into your hair.

Not true. They certainly would not make a nest in the hair of such a dangerous creature. Thanks to echolocation, their amazing ability to avoid objects and swerve and weave away from objects is legendary.

MYTH: Bats are filthy vermin!

While bat roosting areas often have a pile of dark, rice-sized dropping beneath them, the bats themselves always spend time cleaning and grooming themselves when they fly back to their roosts.

Why They Bite

When a bat feels threatened, its natural instinct is to flee or act defensively. The best defensive weapon is their bite and their tiny sharp teeth.

While a bat bite is very rare, a bite by a rabid bat is even rarer.

How They Bite

Being mammals, their skeletal structure includes jaws and teeth. Bats have a unique pattern of teeth with a U-shaped gap separating the upper teeth. However the dental equipment of these insect eaters is very small.

How Afraid Should I Be?

Get some sleep and don't worry about a bat biting you or your loved ones. The likelihood of being bitten by a bat, particularly a rabid bat is far less than you getting hit by a car while the other driver is talking on a cell phone. In the United States, approximately one human dies each year of rabies transmitted by a bat. The odds of being killed by a bat giving you rabies are less than one in a million!

It's true that most of the human rabies cases in the Great Lakes region and the United States are caused by rabies-infected bats. However, more than 99% of bats are rabies-free.

Generally, bats infected with rabies die quickly.

THINK TWICE

Think twice about finding yourself in an attic or other close quarters where bat droppings have accumulated. There is a remote chance of becoming infected with histoplasmosis. This disease is contracted by breathing spores of the fungus Histoplasma capsulatum. It can also be found in bird droppings. The disease usually affects the lungs. Young children and older adults are particularly at risk. If untreated, the disease can be fatal. The best way to prevent it is to stay away from accumulations of bat or bird droppings. If you must frequent such an area, wear a proper respiratory mask.

Preventing Bat Bites

- Do not handle live bats with your bare hands. This is especially true for sick bats—don't mess with them!

- You cannot get rabies simply from seeing a bat or touching its droppings, blood or urine. Nor can you get rabies from touching a bat. Still, it is best not to touch one.

- My preferred method of freeing a bat that somehow finds its way into our house is to sweep it into a butterfly net, just as if I were catching a butterfly. Easier said than done! Once the bat's in the net, I flip the net over so it can't get out. The entangled bat will likely be scared and displeased, and invariably will squeak and show its tiny set of sharp teeth. But I can casually walk the netted bat outside and flip it free.

- If I have to untangle the bat from the fine-meshed net, I put on a pair of leather gloves that the bat's tiny teeth and weak jaws cannot penetrate.

- Keeping bats out of your home reduces the likelihood of a bite. Bats can enter through openings such as cracks, attic vents, rotted holes, loose screens and chimneys. They often choose attics and other outbuildings because such spots are warmer and the crowded conditions are preferred bat nursery sites.

- Caulk or cover all potential openings into your home. Using poisons is not a good idea. The toxin could affect humans or pets, and could result in dead bats rotting in your walls.

bat houses

- Erecting bat houses in your neighborhood also helps divert bats away from your home, while taking advantage of their natural insect control.

Treatment of Bites

- Treat a bat bite as you would a cat or dog bite. Wash the affected area and put an antiseptic on the wound before bandaging it.

- If you are bitten, it is best if you can capture the bat and immediately consult your local health department to have it tested for rabies.

- Pets should have regularly scheduled rabies vaccinations. If you suspect a bat has bitten your unvaccinated pet, try to capture the offending bat and consult your veterinarian.

BOTTOM LINE

Seeing a bat flapping across the evening sky should be cause for celebration at all the mosquitoes and other bugs it's taking down—not a reason to fear. Thanks to its radar-like echolocation, it won't fly into your hair. And the chance of it biting you is extremely remote.

Fish

Bullheads, Muskies and Sunfish . . .Oh My!

I can honestly say I survived a piranha attack when I was bitten on my side while rafting down a wild Costa Rican river. Never mind that it was a 3-inch fish and the bite didn't even break my skin. And never mind that I was back on the raft in record time.

Actually, a greater imprint on my pain index was delivered decades earlier by a lowly, whiskered bullhead just a short bicycle ride from my boyhood home.

About Bullheads and Catfish

This group of fish has no scales and is equipped with whisker-like barbels. In the Great Lakes region they include bullheads, catfish, madtoms and stonecats. There are three bullhead species: black, yellow and brown. Two catfish species reside here, the channel and flathead. Madtoms and closely related stonecats are the smallest members of the catfish clan in our waters.

Found in lakes, creeks and rivers, these fish spend most of their time near the bottom. They have a greater tolerance than most fish for muddy, murky water.

They spawn in the spring and early summer. After the female lays her eggs in shallow water, often in a nest scooped out of the bottom, the male cares for the eggs. After they hatch, one or both of the parents guard the fry (young).

bullhead

muskie

sunfish

About Muskies

Muskies, more properly known as muskellunge, are considered trophy game fish. These large-jawed, toothy predators are at the top of the aquatic food chain. Designed like a torpedo, these long-bodied fish can move fast.

Muskies are most likely to live in warm, weedy lakes, stumpy weed-filled bays and slow-flowing rivers. They spawn in April and May, approximately two weeks after northern pike.

About Sunfish

These panfish are the most common game fish in the Great Lakes region and provide countless hours of angling fun for beginners and experts alike. Common species include bluegill, pumpkinseed and green sunfish. They often hybridize with each other.

Sunfish typically spawn in the late spring and early summer, favoring sand- or gravel-bottomed shallows. They are usually communal spawners, meaning that there will be many nests in a particular area. The female will lay thousands of eggs in a nest fanned out by the male. The male will aggressively defend the plate-sized nest and newly hatched fry.

Their curious nature and opportunistic feeding behavior make them a relatively easy fish to catch for beginners. They often concentrate underneath boat docks and swimming rafts, where they suspend in the shade and feed primarily on invertebrates.

Fascinating Facts

- Unlike bullheads and channel catfish, flatheads feed aggressively on live fish and rarely eat decaying animal matter.

- The world-record muskie weighed more than 69 pounds and was caught in Wisconsin's Chippewa Flowage in 1949.

Thanks to These Fish

- They provide countless hours of fishing recreation for humans.

- They are an important food item for humans and other natural predators.

Myth Busters

MYTH: The whiskers (barbels) of a catfish or bullhead will sting you.

The whiskers or barbels cannot sting you. They are important sensory tools that help these fish detect food in murky water or the dark of night. There are an estimated 100,000 taste buds covering the body of a bullhead; most are concentrated on the barbels.

Why They Bite or Stab

BULLHEADS AND CATFISH

While these fish do not aggressively stab, they do hold their fins straight out when stressed (as when being unhooked), and you are likely to get pricked by the sharp ends if you do not use caution when handling them.

When wading in murky water where you cannot see bottom, it is also a good idea to wear some kind of protective footwear. As a kid, I received a nasty jab while wading barefoot and fishing bullheads.

MUSKIES

Efficient predators, these large, sharp-toothed fish normally eat other fish but will also take small waterfowl, swimming reptiles and amphibians, even small mammals such as mice or muskrats. Since a flash or splash in the water signals a possible meal for a muskie, the splashing of swimming or wading likely incites the rare muskie bite on humans.

SUNFISH

It is not unusual for a sunfish to approach swimmers or waders and nip at their skin. These acts are usually the result of curiosity rather than aggressiveness. The fish might simply be attracted to a spot, such as a small mole, scab or even a hair. Thinking it might be food, they will nip. Though it might be startling, they have no teeth to worry about. The nip will feel like a slight pinch.

How They Bite

BULLHEADS AND CATFISH

Bullheads and catfish possess hard rays (sometimes mistakenly called spines) in their dorsal and pectoral fins. The dorsal is located on the back, while the pectorals are on each side just behind and below the gills. The fish can lock them in place, making it very difficult and unpleasant for predators such as other fish or herons to swallow them. However, the rays are little help against otters and ospreys.

All members of the catfish family native to the Great Lakes region have poison glands associated with the dorsal and pectoral glands, though evidence suggests that for most species, the glands are reduced in size or even disappear as the fish matures. Thus a small channel catfish can deliver toxin but a large one is far

THINK TWICE

Think twice before quickly grabbing a thrashing bullhead that you have just landed. Its hard-rayed dorsal and pectoral fins will be locked in defensive mode and you might be in for a sharp surprise. To handle one, place your palm against its belly and carefully grip the fish, keeping your fingers clear of the fins.

less likely to do so. Madtoms and stonecats, small members of the cat family that look like baby bullheads, produce the most painful toxin, which causes a burning sensation not unlike a bad bee sting. Though the pain can last a few days, the poison is not life threatening.

MUSKIES

A member of the pike family, the muskie sports a duck-like snout and powerful jaws armed with numerous sharp teeth. The lower jaw bristles with large canine teeth, while the upper has short, brush-like teeth. Together, they help the muskie hang onto prey, which are often grabbed with slashing "strikes."

SUNFISH

When a sunfish feeds, or bites, it often makes a cautious approach before sucking in its food in a split-second. It does this by creating a powerful vacuum inside its mouth by springing it open like a small hydraulic trap.

How Afraid Should I Be?

There is no need to be afraid to go swimming in lakes, creeks and rivers. Of the three groups of fish covered here, the sunfish bite is the most common. Muskie bites are extremely rare; statistically, you are more likely to drown while swimming than be bitten by a muskie.

Preventing Fish Jabs, Nips and Bites

BULLHEADS AND CATFISH

- Wear protective footwear such as tennis shoes, water shoes or sandals.

- When fishing, use caution when unhooking fish.

MUSKIES

- Muskies often hunt in weedbeds, so swimming in open water may reduce the likelihood of having your toes mistaken for a meal. Still, our larger-than-perch size is the best prevention. Most muskies and pike do their best to avoid us.

SUNFISH

- When swimming, don't linger near schools of sunfish that are schooled under a raft or dock.

Treatment of Jabs, Nips and Bites

BULLHEADS AND CATFISH

- Wash the pricked site and cover with bandage if necessary.

- Cooling with ice will bring comfort.

- Watch for secondary infections.

MUSKIES

If the bite results in a shallow open wound:

- thoroughly flush and wash the injury

- apply an antiseptic

- if necessary bandage the wound

If the bite is a deep wound:

- seek medical attention

- you might wash the wound and cover the wound temporarily with clean dressing

SUNFISH

The worst that might happen is that a sunfish nip could result in young children becoming frightened to play in the lake. The best thing you can do to downplay a sunfish "attack" is to explain that these are curious little fish and that they are looking for tiny insects for food, and for some reason they think they might find it on our skin.

Better yet, go with the child back into the water and let them nip at you as you explain what is happening. Remember, your behavior will be like an emotional footprint on a child.

BOTTOM LINE

There is no reason to stay on shore because of fish. Yes, on rare occasions a curious sunfish may nip at your skin, but it's not painful and doesn't break the skin. Catfish "jabs" are preventable, and the odds of being bitten by a larger, toothier fish such as a muskie are extremely small.

Rattlesnakes

Nothing motivates people as quickly as the one-syllable word "snake." When someone cries, "SSSnake!" it will likely elicit an immediate, frightened response from others. The very word itself sounds a bit like a hiss.

Snakes are truly one of the premier outcasts in the animal world. Countless myths, untruths and tall tales are floating around out there that simply hang on for generation after generation. We fear snakes, so our children learn to fear snakes. However, by learning more about snakes we can understand their amazing adaptations—and hopefully even begin to admire them.

About Rattlesnakes

The massasauga and the timber rattlesnakes are the only two native poisonous rattlesnakes in the Great Lakes region. The smaller Massasauga has a greater range and is therefore the more common of the two species, but the likelihood of getting bitten by either variety is very, very remote.

massasauga

timber

Life and Times . . .

The timber rattlesnake is the largest rattlesnake in the region. The thick-bodied snake can reach lengths of five feet or more. It has dark bands running across its back, but it can exhibit a range of coloration from yellow to brown, gray or nearly black. The large, wedge-shaped head bears facial pits. The end of the tail is equipped with the characteristic rattle.

The massasauga is smaller, usually less than 30 inches in length. Most of its back is covered with large, dark brown to nearly black spots. The tail is ringed with dark bands rather than spots, and is also tipped with a rattle.

Timber rattlers seek a mate and breed in late summer. They don't mate until they are 5–6 years old and then only every 3–4 years. The female stores sperm in her body during the winter and gives birth the following summer or early fall to a litter of 3–7 baby snakes.

The female massasauga breeds mostly in the spring every 2–4 years and gives birth to 3–20 young in late summer or early fall. Even baby rattlesnakes have small fangs and are capable of injecting a small dose of venom.

Timber rattlesnakes are fond of hibernating in rocky outcroppings on south-facing slopes, while massasaugas often winter near the waterline of wetlands, oftentimes in abandoned crayfish burrows.

Both species of snakes hunt primarily by sitting still and ambushing their prey, which consists of small mammals, birds, frogs and other snakes.

Fascinating Facts

- Like all snakes, rattlesnakes shed their skin approximately once a year. Each time they do so they acquire a new button or rattle on their tail.

- The loud, rapidly vibrating rattle is used to give a clear warning to anything seen as a threat to the snake.

- The U.S. Air Force dubbed its heat-seeking missiles "Sidewinders" in reference to a native rattlesnake of the desert Southwest.

Thanks to Rattlesnakes

- The venom is used to treat certain illnesses and for poison serums.

- These snakes are quite beautiful and to see one (from a safe distance), is a thrilling and unforgettable experience.

- Rattlesnakes feed heavily on crop-damaging rodents. Plus, since snakes are members of a complex natural community, we have yet to discover all of their benefits.

Myth Busters

MYTH: All rattlesnake bites are poisonous.

Approximately a quarter of all timber rattlesnake bites are "dry" bites with no venom injected in the bite.

MYTH: Rattlesnakes will not strike in the dark.

Even in darkness, rattlesnakes can accurately strike. This is due to a pair of sensory pits located on both sides of the face, between the eye and the nostril. This characteristic is what lumps rattlesnakes into the group of snakes known as "pit vipers." Keen, heat-sensing cells located in the pit allow the snake to locate warm-blooded prey in the dark.

Why They Bite

Using poisonous venom to kill prey is a brilliant survival strategy. The poison incapacitates the prey and the predatory snake can easily follow the dying creature and eat it without expending a lot of energy. The poison has a secondary benefit—for self-defense. Hence the snake has venom for only two reasons: to secure food and to defend itself.

How They Bite

Any snake striking at you can be unnerving, but a rattlesnake bite is especially alarming. It happens in less than a second. Due to the fact that this is a venomous snake, it can kill you. But it is unlikely that it will.

The size of the rattlesnake, its age and health determine the potency and amount of venom that is delivered. Of the two species covered here, the timber rattlesnake is far more dangerous than the smaller massasauga.

The bite itself is like a sudden sharp, painful sting. The venom is injected by two specialized teeth called fangs. These teeth can measure nearly an inch long in a big timber rattler. The hollow canal inside the fang delivers the toxin from the venom supply to the tooth. The movable fangs resemble hypodermic needles and are capable of folding back in a sheath of membrane at the roof of the snake's mouth. When the snake strikes, the fangs extend forward to deliver the bite. The snake sheds its fangs every 6–10 weeks.

The venom is a complex blend of chemical compounds. Many are proteins that are basically modified saliva enzymes which help begin the process of digesting prey even before the snake swallows it. The venom attacks the nervous system, particularly nerves that are critical for breathing and blood flow. It can also attack red blood cells and tissues, causing bruising and internal bleeding.

rattlesnake rattle

How Afraid Should I Be?

Approximately 15 people die of snakebites (from rattlesnakes and other venomous snakes) in the United States each year. Bee stings result in many more human deaths. Still, if you suddenly come upon a venomous snake—or any snake for that matter—it might strike at you out of fear.

Preventing Rattlesnake Bites

- Avoid rocky outcroppings, particularly with a southern exposure, where snakes might bask in the sun, particularly in late April and May.

- If you encounter a rattlesnake, it will likely try to crawl away, so be sure to give it a lane of escape. If a snake feels trapped it will typically coil and buzz its tail.

- Move slowly away from any unusual buzzing sound coming from the ground.

- If you know you will be in an area where rattlesnakes are common, you might want to purchase a venom extractor pump, which suctions the poison from the bite.

THINK TWICE

For the most part, snakes are quite secretive and will try to avoid human contact. Think twice about trying to catch a rattlesnake just to show you can do it. And think twice about killing the snake. They do not go around looking for people to bite.

Think twice about getting close to a rattling snake for a photo. Even coiled, they are capable of striking about ⅓ of their body length.

Treatment of Bites

- If someone is bitten, move the person away from the snake and try to keep them calm.

- Lay the victim down with the bite slightly lower than the heart and keep them as still as possible. Remove all rings, bracelets or watches from the affected limb. Wrapping a snug (but not tight) elastic bandage or similar material around the bitten limb just above the bite helps minimize the spread of the poison.

- Seek immediate medical help and get the victim to a medical facility as soon as possible. If possible, call ahead to warn the personnel (to be sure they have Wyeth Crotalidae Antivenin available).

- If you are alone and must go for help, go slowly so as not to exert yourself. With prompt treatment, death is unlikely.

- NEVER cut the snakebite, apply ice to the bite, suck the venom out with your mouth or give any drugs or alcohol to the victim.

BOTTOM LINE

The likelihood of being bitten by either a timber or massaugua rattlesnake is very, very remote. Both species are rare and shy away from humans. If you spot one, enjoy what may be a once-in-a-lifetime sighting and give the snake a wide berth as you leave the immediate area.

Other Snakes

Garter, Hognose, Bull, Fox and Water

As 12-year-olds, my buddy and I would flip over big pieces of scrap wood and sheet metal in hopes of finding a mess of garter snakes. When we saw one, we quickly grabbed it and stuffed it in a burlap sack. Of course we occasionally got bitten. What would you do if some screeching giant pounced on you?

Worse yet, we'd take the writhing sack home to proudly show our catch to other family members—who we knew would get creeped out. We thought it was cool, but we were too young to know that we were reinforcing the universal fear and hatred for this innocent group of animals.

About these Snakes

In the Great Lakes region, most snakes will bite or threaten to bite you if you threaten or mishandle them. For brevity's sake I will briefly cover six species: garter snake, eastern and western hognose snakes (sometimes called "blow snakes"), bullsnake, fox snake and water snake.

Each of these species is non-poisonous.

garter

hognose

bull

fox

northern water

Life and Times . . .

COMMON GARTER SNAKE

This is the most common and widespread snake in the region. It is easily recognized by three yellow stripes that run the length of its body. The background color is black or grayish brown.

Garter snakes will bite if confronted or captured. They thrash wildly when caught and often release their feces and a foul-smelling, musky spray that is potent and not easy to wash off.

HOGNOSE SNAKES

Two species are found here: the eastern and western hognose. Of the two, the eastern type is more common. Its stout body is gray, yellow-brown or even olive brown with a lighter belly. Older snakes may have dark blotches on their backs.

The western hognose is also a stout-bodied snake but it is lighter colored, usually tan or buffy gray. As its name implies it is found in the western part of the Great Lakes region, particularly in open grasslands. Both species have upturned noses, the western variety's is more pronounced.

The hognose is the most frightening appearing of the non-poisonous snakes. When threatened it will flatten out its head like a cobra, hiss loudly and often strike . . . with a closed mouth.

If that doesn't send you down the trail, the snake will roll on its back, open its mouth, hang out its tongue and do a fantastic job of looking dead (see photo at right). The snake's hope is that if it looks dead, you'll leave it alone. Like the garter snake, the hognose also has the ability to discharge a foul-smelling substance that might encourage you to keep your distance.

hognose snake playing dead

BULLSNAKE

This is the longest snake in the Great Lakes region. Adults can measure more than six feet! It is similar to the fox snake, but its head is flecked in yellow with dark spots. A creature of open country, it spends much of its time underground hunting burrowing mammals such as mice and gophers. Consequently it is seldom encountered.

When confronting a person, the snake will likely coil, buzz its tail and hiss loudly. If push comes to shove, a large bullsnake can deliver a painful bite.

FOX SNAKE

Two species are found in the region: the eastern and western fox snake. The western is more common and widespread. Its range includes the western Great Lakes basin from Michigan's Upper Peninsula through Wisconsin and northern Illinois to Minnesota and Iowa. The eastern variety is limited to near-shore areas of lakes Huron and Erie in Michigan, Ohio and Ontario.

The two species are virtually identical, though the western has more dorsal blotches. An average adult fox snake is roughly 3–4 feet long. With its red-brown head and reddish, brown and tan body patterns, it is very well camouflaged.

When disturbed, fox snakes let out a musky smell that is similar to a fox. Hence, the name fox snake.

Unfortunately, folks who think all rattlesnakes should be killed often kill fox snakes as well. The fox snake is often mistaken for a rattler when it rapidly buzzes the tip of its tail. Though it has no rattle, it can make a rattling sound if the tail vibrates against dry leaves or grass.

NORTHERN WATER SNAKE

Water snakes have a dark coloration overall, with dark brown to black bands and blotches on a light brown or gray background. Older snakes appear darker. The belly is white with reddish markings. Adults are 2–4 feet long.

Found in wetlands, water snakes have a very nasty temper when confronted. An agitated snake typically flattens its head, buzzes its tail and strikes, often repeatedly—and sometimes holds on when it bites. Because the snake's saliva contains an anticoagulant, a bite wound might bleed profusely.

Fascinating Facts

- Common Great Lakes toads such as the American toad have a pair of parotoid glands behind their eyes that discharge a toxin that makes them very distasteful to most animals. The garter and eastern hognose snakes must consider the poison like a fine sauce, because they love eating toads!

- A breastbone called the sternum connects our ribs. Snakes do not have sternums. Their "floating ribs" allow them to move sinuously and to swallow items larger than their own head.

Thanks to Snakes

- They often feed on insects and small rodents that can be harmful to agricultural crops.

- All snakes play an important role in the natural environment by contributing to ecological systems as predators and prey.

Myth Busters

MYTH: A snake's tongue is poisonous!

Not true. The tongue is a sensory organ used to detect smells. It picks up scent molecules and brushes them across a special organ on the roof of the mouth called a Jacobson's organ.

MYTH: A snake can grip the tip of its tail with its mouth and roll away for a fast escape or to pursue their prey.

garter snake

Snakes do NOT roll like a wheel. They crawl. The most common locomotion is called lateral undulation. The snake creates a series of waves of bending their body from head to tail. When the bend contacts an object such as rock or stick it pushes against it helping it to move forward or laterally. When the series of waves push against objects at the same time, the snake moves forward.

MYTH: Snakes are slimy!

This is a common misconception. Often aligned with amphibians, which can have moist, slimy skin, snakes and other reptiles are covered with small dry scales. The scales, particularly the larger belly scales, are smooth and often shiny making them appear wet.

THINK TWICE

Think twice about picking up a snake. Unless you catch it properly and handle it gently, you might be bitten.

Why They Bite

All of the snakes mentioned above will always try their best to avoid confrontations with humans. Flight and camouflage are their primary means of escape. However, if captured or cornered they often strike and bite.

How They Bite

None of these snakes have sharp fangs. Though their recurved teeth are sharp, they are quite small.

How Afraid Should I Be?

No need to be afraid. None of these snakes are poisonous, nor do any of them have large teeth. Some of the larger snakes might break your skin with a bite, but it will be shallow and may not even bleed.

If you or other family members handle reptiles you need to be aware that nearly all reptiles carry Salmonella bacteria in their intestinal tract and they often shed these bacteria in their feces. While not causing illness in the reptile, they can cause serious illness in people. Most exposures result in diarrhea, fever and abdominal cramps. However if it spreads to the bloodstream, bone marrow or nervous system, the infection can be serious and sometimes fatal.

For the bacteria to spread to humans, fingers or objects that have been contaminated with reptile feces must be placed in the mouth.

Prevention from Salmonella infection is easy. ALWAYS wash your hands with hot soapy water after handling reptiles (snakes, lizards and turtles).

Preventing Snake Bites

- Don't crowd a snake. If you appear threatening, it might bite.

Treatment of Bites

- It's okay to let out a "yikes!" but that is usually all you will have to do.

- If the bite breaks your skin, wash the wound and cover it with a bandage if necessary. Watch it over the course of a few days for the possibility of a secondary infection.

BOTTOM LINE

There's no need to be afraid of garter, bull, hognose and water snakes. They will do everything in their power to avoid you, and bites from undisturbed snakes are very rare. Even if you manage to accidentally corner or upset one, these snakes are not poisonous and do not have large teeth.

Skunks

It was mid-March and as we were driving back to Aunt Angeline's farm one evening, we had our car windows open a crack. In the darkness we came to a point where the unmistakable smell of the first skunk of the spring wafted into the car. Aunt Angeline inhaled deeply and with great satisfaction she declared, "Ahh, there's nothing like a two-toned kitty with fluid drive!"

About Skunks

Two species of skunks live in the Great Lakes area. These are the widespread striped skunk and the rare and smaller eastern spotted skunk, which appears to be in a decline in this region. Given that striped skunks are far more numerous we will discuss their life history.

Life and Times . . .

If you want attention, make a noise or dress wildly. In a world where most animals wear subdued colors so that they might better blend in with the countryside, skunks do not follow the rules. Their message is a loud and clear "HEY, LOOK AT ME! HERE I AM!"

These distinctly striped, black-and-white cat-sized mammals are primarily nocturnal so we rarely encounter them.

When we do, it is usually in spring, summer and fall. During the winter months these quiet mammals den up; sometimes sharing a den with up to a dozen fellow skunks. Such cuddling helps conserve energy. Even so, they often lose half their body weight in winter.

Skunks are most commonly found in farmland or semi-open areas. They tend to avoid forests. Active at night, they den up during the day in old woodchuck and badger burrows, and underneath rock piles, hollow trees or outbuildings. I remember discovering a skunk when a boyhood buddy and I flipped over an old car hood lying on the ground. We were looking for snakes but discovered a startled skunk!

When skunks emerge from their winter dormancy in late winter and early spring, they set off to find a mate. This is the only time of the year that adult males and females are found together. After mating in March and April, two months pass before the female gives birth to 4–6 babies (kittens). They stay with her for up to a year but are capable of breeding at 10 months of age.

Skunks are omnivores, feeding both on plants and animals. Like raccoons they are quite opportunistic. They will feed on human garbage, bird eggs and even carrion. Since they often eat beetle grubs, ants and other underground insects, their front claws—longer than the back claws—are perfect tools for digging. Skunk diggings are common signs of their whereabouts.

Fascinating Facts

- All members of the weasel family (Mustelidae) have well-developed anal scent glands. Their function is for scent-marking territorial boundaries and for defense. Hands down, of all the weasel family, skunks have the most spectacular scent glands.

- Skunks and raccoons are the most common mammals to be found infected with rabies.

Thanks to Skunks

- Skunks, particularly young ones, are a food item for great horned owls, foxes, coyotes and bobcats.

- They are an important component to the rich biodiversity of the Great Lakes region.

Myth Busters

MYTH: If your dog gets sprayed, give it a bath in tomato juice.

This old wives' tale has been around for some time. What really happens is that when your nose is subject to a high dose of skunk spray, you develop what is called olfactory fatigue. This means that your nose quits smelling the odor. Instead, you can easily smell the tomato juice and convince yourself that the skunk smell has been washed away. Someone coming upon the scene will gasp and tell you that the skunk smell is awful.

Why They Bite or Spray

When a skunk feels threatened it will either lope away or it will lift its tail straight up, with all tail hair erect to give the tail as much notice as possible. The message is, "Watch it! Don't bother me!" Its other defensive weapons are their sharp teeth and bite. While a skunk bite is very rare, a bite by a rabid skunk is even more uncommon.

How They Bite (And in this case, spray!)

Like other carnivorous mammals, skunks have four sharp canine teeth and scissor-like shearing premolars called *carnassials* (last upper premolars and first lower molars).

These are adaptations for killing, cutting and tearing meat. Clearly these same tools can be used as defensive weapons, and they are capable of delivering a nasty bite.

With such short, stubby legs, it isn't easy for a skunk to outrun a predator. The striped skunk has developed a unique defense system. When a skunk is threatened, it first tries to run away from the predator. If that doesn't work, it tries to frighten the attacker by arching its back, raising its tail and turning its back on the threat. It may also stomp its feet. If this doesn't work, as a last resort, the skunk will spray the animal with a strong-smelling fluid. The fluid really stinks and can also sting the predator's eyes—giving the skunk time to get away. A skunk can spray as far as twelve feet!

THINK TWICE

Think twice about moving in to get the perfect photo of a skunk. If necessary, the skunk can spray its noxious delivery up to 12 feet!

How Afraid Should I Be?

It is highly unlikely you or your family will be faced with a skunk bite. A potentially dangerous skunk is one that becomes unafraid of humans. Normally these are shy, non-aggressive animals.

You should be suspicious of any skunk that is:

- acting unusual, bold or aggressive
- moving about during daylight hours
- walking irregularly, almost as if it were drunk

If it displays one of these symptoms, there is a slight chance that it has rabies.

Non-Bite Concerns

Far and away the greatest fear in dealing with skunks is their chemical warfare weaponry. Being sprayed or even being in the vicinity of a skunk spraying is truly an unforgettable experience. Of course, the skunk is hoping that you will not forget it and perhaps next time you will give it a wide berth!

If a skunk sprays you, it can cause nausea and a burning of your eyes. At the very least, you will likely find the encounter aromatically unpleasant!

The skunk's spray is a yellow oil composed of chemical compounds called thiols. These contain sulphur. The foul concoction is stored in two prune-sized glands with openings in the skunk's anus.

Prior to spraying, the skunk will turn its rear end to face the threat (you!) and lift its plume-like tail straight up. The message at this point is a very clear, "Okay this is a warning! Back off!"

Preventing Skunk Bites or Spray Episodes

- The best advice is to simply steer clear of wild skunks. Do not feed them or try to approach them. And if one tries to approach you or its tail stands up, move away!

Treatment of Bites and Spray Blasts

- Treat a skunk bite as you would a cat or dog bite. If the wound is severe, seek medical attention. Since it is a wild animal you should contact the proper animal control agency and your doctor or department of health for further advisement. These animals should be tested for rabies virus after biting humans.

- If you have been sprayed by a skunk, take off your clothes outside your home to prevent it from being "skunked." To remove skunk odor from your clothes or clean-up towels, wash them with one cup of liquid laundry bleach per gallon of water.

- Take a very long, soapy shower!

- If your dog or cat has been sprayed, bathe the animal in a mixture of 1 quart of 3% hydrogen peroxide (purchase at a drug store), ¼ cup of baking soda (sodium bicarbonate) and a teaspoon of liquid detergent. After five minutes of bathing, rinse your pet with water and repeat bathing if necessary. Be careful to keep the solution out of the pet's eyes and mouth.

- To be effective, the mixture must be fresh, not stored. Note that the mixture might temporarily bleach your pet's hair.

- Products such as Skunk-Off are available for "deodorizing" pets. Carefully follow the directions, and keep in mind that none of these remedies works as well as time. Over the course of two to three weeks, the compounds in the spray will break down on their own.

BOTTOM LINE

It's highly unlikely you or your family will be bitten by a skunk. Normally these are shy, non-aggressive animals. You are much more likely to be sprayed. While unpleasant, this is also a rare occurrence if you give skunks a wide berth—especially if one raises its tail!

Snapping Turtles

Snapping turtles have an image problem. Even their name, "snapping," indicates aggressiveness. They are not cute. In fact, they are quite homely and their nature is one of a grumpy old man.

As youngsters, my friends and I used to spend summers swimming in an abandoned gravel pit. A rarely seen, giant snapping turtle we called "*Old Moses*" lived at the pit. This snapper became a legend and more than once while swimming, one of my buddies would scream out, "It's *Old Moses*! I felt him with my foot!!" Like junior Olympians we would race out of the water to the security of dry land, where we would catch our breath glad that we had escaped with all of our toes. Little did we know that unprovoked snappers will not bite toes while in the water.

About Snapping Turtles

Snapping turtles are significantly larger than other Great Lakes region turtles. Thirty to 60 pounds is not uncommon and a 75-pounder is a giant!

snapping turtle

The snapping turtle has successfully managed to live on earth much longer than humans, and has adapted to survive in almost any freshwater aquatic habitat.

It is an omnivore, eating both plant and animal material. An excellent scavenger and stealthy hunter, it hunts by sitting still on the bottom of the wetland and ambushing its prey.

spiny softshell turtle

Another turtle of the Great Lakes Region that can be aggressive is the soft-shelled turtle. Easily recognized by its smooth, rubbery shell and long, pig-like nose, it is shy and rarely encountered. Like the snapping turtle, it is occasionally caught while fishing. When scared—as in being pulled into a boat—it most likely will try to bite you. It is best to free the turtle by simply cutting the line.

Life and Times . . .

Mating takes place at about five years of age. Typically in May or June, the female scoops out a hole with one of her back legs, deposits up to 40 round, white eggs, covers them up and leaves them. The warmth of the sun on the soil will incubate the eggs.

In roughly 2½ months, the eggs hatch and the hatchling turtles must dig their way out of the nest. Sometimes in the northerly areas like the Great Lakes region, eggs may overwinter and hatch the following spring.

The hatchlings are never more vulnerable in their life than when they must make the oftentimes lengthy journey from their birth nest to the water.

Fascinating Facts

- Since these turtles spend so much time in the water, their shells are often covered in green algae. Other species, like painted turtles, bask in the sun more often making it difficult for algae to grow.

- Similar to other species of turtles, the temperature of the soil covering the buried eggs determines the sex of snapping turtles. Warmer soil temperatures tend to favor producing females.

- Snappers are capable of living for decades, much longer than most animals. The average life span of a snapping turtle is estimated at 30–40 years.

Thanks to Snapping Turtles

- Snapping turtles are important members of the cleanup crew in aquatic communities. Falsely accused of having a negative affect on fish populations, they actually help keep fisheries healthy by feeding on sick, injured or dead fish.

- Turtle eggs and hatchlings are often food items for raccoons, skunks, foxes, coyotes, herons and other predators.

Myth Busters

MYTH: The snapping turtle will bite off your finger or toe if it grabs you!

Though they make a lunging, audible hiss and snap, it is highly unlikely that one will sever any of your digits. The larger the turtle and the more you struggle, however, the more likely you are to experience an open wound.

Why They Bite

Snapping turtles try their best to avoid humans, and only bite when they feel threatened. Most bites occur when the turtle is out of the water.

How They Bite

As with other turtles, this reptile has no teeth. Instead, the turtle's mouth resembles a beak. Its sharp edges cut and shear food items ranging from crayfish and fish to salamanders, snails and plants. Therefore a turtle bite is capable of cutting you. To defend itself, a snapping turtle will turn to face its attacker; be forewarned, it can extend its neck half the length of its upper shell!

How Afraid Should I Be?

This is one of those animals whose myth is greater than its bite. In reality, this primitive reptile is not anywhere near the threat it is perceived to be. Turtle bites are extremely rare and they do not happen in the water. However, a bite is likely on land—if you put yourself too close to the mouth of a frightened turtle.

THINK TWICE

Think twice about picking up a snapping turtle to take home as a pet. They do not make good pets and handling it puts you at greater risk of being on the receiving end of a bite.

Think twice about taking turtle eggs from a nest. Moving them to another location threatens their survival.

Preventing Snapping Turtle Bites

- You can swim worry-free because they will NOT bite you in the water unless you are very careless and posing a threat to them. They will NOT pursue swimmers.

- When you encounter a snapping turtle out of the water, simply keep your distance and do not harass the turtle with sticks and other objects. Annoyed turtles are more likely to bite in their own defense.

Treatment of Bites

If a turtle bites you and holds on, do not attempt to pull away. It will let go on its own. Admittedly your first response is to pull away, but if you do, you increase the risk of the bite cutting you. Try to stay calm, grit your teeth and patiently wait for the turtle to release its grip. If you receive a cut, wash it with clean water and soap, bandage it and seek medical attention if necessary.

BOTTOM LINE

Snapping turtles are nowhere near the threat people perceive them to be. Bites are extremely rare and only happen when the turtle feels threatened. Enjoy sightings of this prehistoric-looking animal from a respectful distance, and do not put yourself anywhere near its mouth. A snapping turtle can and will extend its neck the length of its shell to defend itself.

Raccoons

"There is a beast they call aroughcun ["he who scratches with his hands"], much like a badger, but useth to live [in] trees as squirrels do. Their squirrels some are near as great as our smallest sort of wild rabbits, some blackish or black and white, but the most are gray."

-Captain John Smith, author of *Generall Historie of Virginia* (1624)

About Raccoons

There are more raccoons in the Great Lakes region today than there were 200 years ago. This adaptable mammal—whose brand is the distinctive black "mask" over its eyes and its fluffy, black-ringed tail—is both loved and scorned. Like a bandit, it can steal your heart or your picnic.

Though its long, sharp canine teeth clearly lump it into the mammalian order *Carnivora*, the raccoon is an omnivore that eats a broad range of foods and will not pass up an opportunity to fill its belly.

Its keen hearing, excellent night vision and amazing sense of touch are all adaptations for the nightlife it favors over daytime adventures.

Life and Times . . .

Raccoons prefer to live near trees and water. Though more common in stands of deciduous trees than conifers, this highly adaptable animal is comfortable living in both urban and wild environments. It is not unusual to find raccoons in an abandoned house or barn.

One reason this opportunistic mammal is so widespread is its wide range of foods. An omnivore, it eats fruits, nuts, seeds, garden crops such as corn and watermelons, insects, bird eggs, crayfish, fish, frogs, small rodents, human trash and carrion (particularly road-killed animals).

In the Great Lakes region, males, which are slightly larger than females, begin to look for a mate in February, with mating peaking in March. After roughly 65 days of pregnancy, the female gives birth to 3–7 young.

After a month or so, the young leave their birthing den and join the mother in foraging for food. They will stay with their mother through their first winter before heading out on their own the following spring. One-year-old females are capable of breeding and producing young.

Raccoons usually den alone but during their winter dormancy (not true hibernators) they often share denning quarters. This cuddling behavior conserves heat and helps them survive the long winter. In northern regions, a raccoon's body fat in late fall might account for half of its total weight. By winter's end, most of this fat is burned off.

Fascinating Facts

- Related to coatis and ringtails, the raccoon is the only member of the Procyonidae family found in the Great Lakes region. (Procyon is Latin for "before dogs." This refers to the point that the raccoon's ancestors have been around longer than those of dogs and wolves.)

- Some Native Americans referred to the raccoon as the "bear's little brother." Like a bear, it walks on all four feet with an arch in its back, and has non-retractable claws. And like humans and bears, the raccoon walks using the entire sole of the foot "heel to toe."

- Their clawed feet, each bearing five toes, help make them excellent tree climbers. Their reasonably long tail serves as an aid in balance.

Thanks to Raccoons

- The fur of raccoons has been harvested for clothing for centuries.

- Raccoons are a food item for other wildlife such as coyotes. They are also a food source for some people.

- They are an important component to the rich biodiversity of the Great Lakes region.

Myth Busters

MYTH: Raccoons always wash their food before eating it.

While this might be good advice for us, it is not the case with raccoons.

Their species name *lotor* means "washer," but raccoons do not always dunk their food, even when near water, and will not hesitate to eat when water is not nearby. Biologists are unsure as to why raccoons have this strange habit.

Why They Bite

When threatened, the raccoon's natural instinct is to flee or act defensively. The best defensive weapons are its sharp teeth and strong bite. While a raccoon bite is very rare, a bite by a rabid raccoon is even rarer.

How They Bite

Like other carnivorous mammals, raccoons have four sharp canine teeth and scissor-like shearing premolars called *carnassial* teeth (last upper premolars and first lower molars).

These are adaptations for killing, cutting and tearing meat. Clearly they can also be used as defensive weapons. With their quickness, relatively strong jaws and sharp teeth, they are capable of delivering a nasty bite.

THINK TWICE

Think twice about keeping a baby raccoon for a pet. In fact it may be illegal for you to keep one as a pet without a proper permit.

Think twice about feeding a raccoon. Putting your hand in front of any wild animal's mouth is never a good idea. A seemingly harmless situation could turn into a nervous bite delivered by the raccoon.

How Afraid Should I Be?

It is unlikely you or your family will be faced with a raccoon bite. A potentially dangerous raccoon is one that becomes unafraid of humans. Normally these are shy, non-aggressive animals. You should be suspicious of any raccoon that is acting bold or aggressive. There is a slight chance that it is infected with rabies.

Non-Bite Concerns

RABIES

Only mammals are affected by the rabies virus, which is carried in the saliva. Rabies is a serious infection of the nervous system. If not treated quickly, it is capable of making a person very ill and death can result.

Rabies is occasionally found in raccoons. In the United States, more than 7,000 animals (wild and domestic) annually are diagnosed with rabies. It is usually transmitted by a bite. Though non-bite infections are rare, it is possible for infected saliva to enter the eyes, nose, mouth or an open wound.

Avoid contact with any raccoon that displays unusual, bold or sickly behavior. Animals that have rabies are often described as "foaming at the mouth." This happens because the animal's nerves no longer work properly and it can't swallow its own saliva. If you find a dead raccoon, do not handle it with bare hands. For more on rabies, see page 8.

RACCOON ROUNDWORM (*BAYLISASCARIS PROCYONIS*)

Though not a bite, a roundworm found in the feces of some raccoons can cause misery in humans. Raccoons are the primary host of this roundworm, which is commonly found in their small intestines. If they infect a human, the microscopic, migrating roundworms can cause skin irritations, as well as eye and brain damage. There have been less than a handful of human deaths, all of them children, but nonetheless one should be aware of the possibility of transmission.

Raccoon feces can carry millions of roundworm eggs. Humans can encounter the eggs through contact with raccoon droppings or by touching a contaminated area or object (the eggs persist long after the feces disappear). Small children are especially vulnerable because they often put their fingers, objects or even droppings into their mouth. Any area contaminated with raccoon feces should be cleaned and the feces burned, along with any affected feed, straw, hay or other materials.

Preventing Raccoon Bites or Roundworm

- The best advice is to not approach wild raccoons or let them approach you.

- To prevent a roundworm infection, minimize contact with any area inhabited by raccoons. Roundworm eggs are very resistant to environmental conditions and can survive for several years. Children and pets should be kept away from these contaminated areas until a thorough cleaning has occurred. It is important to keep decks and picnicking areas around your home clean of food scraps, as these might attract raccoons.

Treatment of Bites

- Basically treat a raccoon bite as you would a cat or dog bite. If the wound is severe, seek medical attention. Since it is a wild animal you should contact the proper animal control agency and your doctor or department of health for further advisement.

- Puncture wounds should be thoroughly flushed and cleaned with a topical antibiotic. Deep wounds require medical assistance.

- Watch for possible infection of the bite site.

- Rabies is treatable through a series of vaccination shots. Every year approximately 40,000 people in the United States receive these shots as a precaution.

- A valid tetanus shot is a good idea.

- Roundworm treatment is very difficult. If you have been exposed, or even suspect exposure to raccoon roundworm, seek immediate medical care. Currently no drugs can effectively kill the larvae moving in the body. Laser surgery has been used to successfully treat larvae present in the retina, but eye damage caused by migrating larvae is irreversible. Treatment with steroids can help decrease inflammatory reactions.

BOTTOM LINE

The chances of you or a member of your family being bitten by a raccoon are remote. Still, a raccoon that is sick, injured or has become unafraid of humans is a potentially dangerous animal. Reduce your risk by not approaching raccoons or allowing them to approach you—especially ones that are acting bold or aggressive.

Coyotes

A long, long time ago, people did not yet inhabit the Earth. A monster walked upon the land, eating all the animals—except Coyote.

Realizing that Coyote was sly and clever, the monster thought of a new plan. It would befriend Coyote and invite him to stay in its home. Before the visit began, Coyote said that he wanted to visit his friends and asked if he could enter the monster's stomach to see them. The monster allowed this, and Coyote cut out its heart and set fire to its insides. His friends were freed.

—Nez Perce Indian story called *Coyote and Monster*

About Coyotes

Among many North American Indian tribes, coyotes held a special place in oral storytelling. Taking the role of "trickster," the coyote established itself as a very special animal.

Though coyotes originally branched out from the open grasslands and deserts of the southwestern United States they have spread all across North America. In the Great Lakes region, coyotes are increasing. Extremely adaptable, they are sometimes found living within city limits.

Life and Times . . .

These wild members of the dog family are highly social animals. They are most active at dawn and sunset, though it is not unusual to hear family groups yapping and howling throughout the evening. This does not mean that they are making a kill; it could simply be a means of "singing" and reinforcing their family unit.

Despite their preference for hunting during low-light periods, they can be seen at any time of the day. If you spot one, there is a good chance that others are nearby.

Resembling a small German Shepherd with sharp, pointed ears, the average coyote weighs 20–40 pounds. The muzzle is slender and narrow, more like a fox than a wolf. When a coyote runs, its black-tipped tail droops below its back. Dogs and wolves typically run with their tails level to upright.

A coyote pair may stay together for life. The female comes into her estrus cycle (comes into heat) once a year, sometime from January into March, and mating occurs over a period of 4–5 days. The pups, averaging 5–7 per litter, are born about two months later in an underground den.

Coyotes are so widespread because of their ability to eat almost anything and to cope so well with humans. They can be found in almost any habitat. Wild foods include small rodents, rabbits, hares, squirrels, birds, insects, fruit, reptiles, amphibians and occasionally deer (usually road-killed, crippled or sick deer) Non-wild foods include garden produce, domestic cats, dogs and small livestock, and abundant human garbage.

Humans have removed most of the coyote's traditional predators, which included grizzly and black bears, mountain lions and wolves. Some of these species are increasing, but only in localized areas and not widespread. While humans have unknowingly played a major role in the success and spread of coyotes, we are also their major enemy.

Fascinating Facts

- Coyotes occasionally mate with domestic dogs. Their young are referred to as "coydogs." Coydogs generally do not make good pets, however, as they are more nervous than dogs and therefore more likely to bite.

- Coyotes can actually run faster than a roadrunner! They can run 40 miles per hour and leap an 8-foot fence.

- Like your pet dog, coyotes maintain their territories by scent-marking (peeing along boundaries), howling and barking.

- The scientific name for coyote, *Canis latrans*, mean "barking dog." Coyotes communicate through howling, yelping, barking, and huffing. Howling is used to communicate with other coyotes in the area. It is generally used to declare territorial rights. It is also an invitation for females to join the howling male.

Yelping sounds wildly exuberant and it is, in a sense, a form of celebration of an assembled pack or it is heard in play. Barking is usually a threat display when a coyote is possessing its kill or guarding its den. Lastly, though rarely heard by humans, is huffing. It is usually softly delivered to call coyote pups without drawing attention of nearby predators such as wolves or humans.

Thanks to Coyotes

- The fur of coyotes has been harvested for clothing for hundreds if not thousands of years.

- Coyotes feed heavily on many small rodents, squirrels and woodchucks that are sometimes pests to agricultural crops.

- They are an important component of the rich biodiversity of the Great Lakes region.

Myth Busters

MYTH: We have both brush wolves and coyotes around here.

Both titles refer to the same species. The label "brush wolves" is frequently used in the Great Lakes region and was once more commonly used than coyote. Coyotes found in more northerly regions tend to be larger and heavier than their southern counterparts.

MYTH: Coyotes kill mostly game animals.

Research shows that coyotes in both urban and rural areas feed primarily on rodents. However, if given the opportunity they will not turn down a white-tailed deer fawn or a clutch of pheasant eggs. And as Canada geese have flourished, some coyotes have learned to flush geese off their nests and steal the eggs.

THINK TWICE

Think twice if you're tempted to feed a coyote. By feeding it you are reinforcing behavior that will create a nuisance animal and likely shorten its life. And you are increasing the odds of being bitten.

Why They Bite

While thousands of dog bites are treated each year in the Great Lakes region, coyote bites are extremely rare.

The natural instinct for a coyote that feels threatened is to flee or act defensively. Its best defensive weapon is its sharp teeth and bite. While a coyote bite is very rare, a bite by a rabid coyote is even less common.

Animals that have become habituated to, or grown comfortable around and unafraid of humans, deliver almost all coyote bites. Often found around campgrounds and picnic areas, these coyotes should not be trusted.

How They Bite

Like other carnivorous mammals, coyotes have four sharp canine teeth and scissor-like shearing premolars called *carnassials* (last upper premolars and first lower molars).

These are adaptations for killing, cutting and tearing meat, but they can also be used in self-defense. With their quickness, relatively strong jaws and sharp teeth, coyotes are capable of delivering a nasty bite.

How Afraid Should I Be?

It is unlikely you or your family will be faced with a coyote bite. A potentially dangerous coyote is one that becomes unafraid of humans. Normally these are shy, secretive animals. Most coyote bites happen in areas where they have become habituated to humans; particularly where humans are feeding them. You should be suspicious of any coyote that is acting bold or aggressive.

RABIES

Rabies has not been found in coyotes in the Great Lakes region, but it is still a possibility. For more information on rabies risks and precautions, see page 8.

Preventing Coyote Bites

- Never approach or attempt to touch a coyote.

- Discourage coyotes from hanging around your home. Uneaten food attracts unwanted visitors, including coyotes. Keep food garbage cleaned up. Make composted foods unavailable through proper screening, or place them in an enclosed composter.

- Keep small to mid-size pets indoors, and if you feed larger pets outdoors, be sure that all uneaten food is cleaned up.

Treatment of Bites

- Treat a coyote bite like you would a cat or dog bite. If the wound is severe, seek medical attention. Since it is a wild animal, you should contact the proper animal control agency and your doctor or department of health for further advisement.

- Puncture wounds should be thoroughly flushed and cleaned with a topical antibiotic. Deep puncture wounds require medical assistance.

- Watch for possible infection of the bite site.

BOTTOM LINE

Most coyotes avoid humans and attacks are extremely rare. The few bites reported have nearly always involved animals that have grown comfortable around—and unafraid of—humans. Coyotes hanging around campgrounds and picnic areas where ill-advised feeding occurs should not be trusted.

Gray Wolves

If you were assigned to brand or market the idea of wilderness, you would likely consider the gray wolf as one of its symbols. It is an amazing animal that displays strength, perseverance, loyalty and teamwork.

For centuries, humans have had a love-hate relationship with the gray wolf. Native Americans considered the animal a sign of strength, cunning and a good provider, while early European settlers saw the wolf as a threat to the opening of the wilderness.

About Gray Wolves

The gray wolf or timber wolf has actually been increasing in recent years, and the Great Lakes region is home to the greatest number of wolves in the continental United States, with somewhere around 4,000 animals.

Life and Times . . .

The gray wolf is the largest member of the wild dog family in North America. Weighing up to 130 pounds, it is typically much larger than a coyote, with longer legs (but shorter ears).

Male wolves are slightly larger than females. Both are highly social animals and live in packs. The pack is made up of the breeding pair (known as the "alpha" pair), their pups and other non-breeding adult wolves. A wolf's ability to survive depends on the strength of the pack. Not only are they a family unit, but they also cooperate to hunt, raise young and defend their territory (50–1,000 square miles) from other packs and individual wolves.

Capable of breeding at 2–3 years, gray wolves sometimes mate for life.

After breeding in January and February, an average of 5 pups are born in early spring. Like other mammals, the pups depend on their mother's milk for the first part of their lives. After weaning, the pups are fed regurgitated meat brought back by members of the pack. At about 8 months, the young wolves are running and hunting with the adults.

As carnivores, they eat a range of animals, including deer, moose, beavers, hares, mice and assorted other small mammals.

Fascinating Facts

- When hunting, wolves might travel 30 miles in a day. They trot along at five miles per hour but can sprint up to 40 miles per hour for short distances.

- Why do wolves howl? Biologists have learned that wolves howl not to simply communicate. Sometimes they simply like to howl—kind of like singing in the shower!

- Howling also reinforces pack unity and harmony. It might announce the start or end of a hunt, or sound a warning to other wolves—both in their own and neighboring packs.

Thanks to Gray Wolves

- Besides being a prominent symbol of the wilderness, these amazing creatures are always a popular species of wildlife for humans to hear, watch and photograph.

- They are an important component to the rich biodiversity of the Great Lakes region and a key player in predator-prey relationships.

Myth Busters

MYTH: Wolves are devastating to our deer herd.

A wolf kills about 18 deer per year to survive. Assuming there are roughly 4,000 wolves in Minnesota, Wisconsin and Michigan, then we could estimate that 72,000 deer are killed to feed wolves. By comparison, conservatively 140,000 deer are killed in vehicle collisions each year in these three states. And human hunters easily account for more than one million deer annually.

Why They Bite

Wolves will usually go out of their way to avoid humans and are rarely a threat to us. Most reported attacks on humans involved wolves that had been fed by people and had become habituated. Wolves are wild animals and should be treated as such. There will always be cases of a "bad apple" wolf. Just as there are some bad people, there can be ill-tempered or unusual wolves.

How They Bite

Like other carnivorous mammals, wolves have four sharp canine teeth and scissor-like shearing premolars called *carnassials* (last upper premolars and first lower molars). These are adaptations for killing, cutting and tearing food, but work well as defensive weapons. With their quickness, strong jaws and sharp teeth, wolves are capable of inflicting a nasty bite.

How Afraid Should I Be?

THINK TWICE

Think twice if you see what appears to be a tame wolf in a state or national park. Though it may appear tame, it is still a wild animal and will be unpredictable.

There is absolutely no need to be afraid. To my knowledge there have been no wild wolf bites in the Great Lakes region. Most accounts of "wolf attacks" were cases where the wolves were feeding on a human who had died of other causes.

On the other hand, any wild wolf or other wild animal that has become used to humans and allows hand feeding is one to worry about.

Preventing Gray Wolf Bites

- Never approach or attempt to touch a wolf.

- To discourage wolves from hanging around your home, keep small pets indoors. If you feed pets outdoors, be sure that all uneaten food is put away. Keep garbage cleaned up, and make composted foods unavailable through proper screening, or place them in an enclosed composter.

Treatment of Bites

- If you are bitten by a wolf, contact the proper animal control agency or local conservation officer and your doctor or department of health.

- Treat it as you would a cat or dog bite. Puncture wounds should be thoroughly flushed and cleaned with a topical antibiotic. Deep punctures and other serious wounds require medical assistance.

- Watch for possible infection of the bite site.

BOTTOM LINE

Wolves will go out of their way to avoid humans. Your chances of even seeing one in the Great Lakes area are so small, you should consider yourself extremely lucky if you do.

Black Bears

Among indigenous human cultures, few wild animals have held such a place of honor as the black bear. They were held sacred and to be offered "bear medicine" was a highly revered gift. Perhaps we need to resurrect the concept of "bear medicine;" to practice introspection and take in all the facts, give it critical thought and then act.

I had not originally intended to include the black bear in this book. However, when I surveyed outdoor professionals and enthusiasts about which creatures to cover, the black bear kept popping up as an animal that strikes fear into the hearts of many folks. You know the familiar mantra, "Lions and tigers and bears. Oh, my!" We have grown up with this fear constantly being taught to us.

Perhaps we need to resurrect the concept of "bear medicine."

About Black Bears

The only wild bear living in the Great Lakes region is the black bear. These large omnivores are opportunistic feeders that not only eat wild foods such as plants, fruit, fish, insects and small mammals, but also will take advantage of human garbage, birdseed and yes, even camp food.

With the recent increase in black bear numbers, it is becoming more of a common occurrence to see one of these magnificent beasts. Yet the greatest threat to black bears is loss of habitat. As humans continue to build homes and cabins in bear country, the likelihood of a bear/human conflict increases.

Life and Times . . .

True to their name, black bears are usually black, though occasionally they are brown, tan or cinnamon. These large, mostly secretive mammals prefer forest or mixed farmland/forest living.

During the winter months, black bears are specialized hibernators. They usually den up for winter in October and November. Unlike some mammal hibernators, such as the woodchuck or ground squirrel, the bear's winter body temperature does not change dramatically from its summer body temp.

In January or February, a pregnant female bear gives birth to 2–3 cubs. She nurses them on nutritious milk, rich in fats, which she produces from her stores of body fat. Cubs generally stay with their mother for two winters before going off on their own.

By the end of March, bears are on the move and begin looking for food. Their mating season is in early summer around the month of June. The bears' primary job in summer and early fall is to eat and eat.

Fascinating Facts

- The black bear is the most widespread of the three North American bear species. The other two are grizzly or brown and the polar bear.

- The black bear is the only North American bear that often climbs trees.

- While an adult human male might consume an average of 1,500 calories per day, the black bear can consume 30,000 calories per day during late summer and early fall while preparing for its winter hibernation.

- Bears and dogs are close relatives. Taxonomists believe that they shared a common ancestor.

- A bear's normal heartbeat on a summer day is 50–90 beats per minute. During hibernation, it only beats about 8 times a minute!

Thanks to Black Bears

- Besides being a prominent symbol of wild regions, these large mammals are always a popular species of wildlife for humans to watch. Being omnivores, they will not pass up scavenging on dead animals.

Myth Busters

MYTH: If you encounter a black bear, particularly a mother and cubs, you will be attacked.

There is a common legend that black bears, especially black bear mothers, attack any humans they see. That's simply not true. Black bears very rarely attack. It's highly unlikely they will attack you, even if you are near a mother and her cubs. But that doesn't mean you should take the chance. If you see any black bears keep to a safe distance. They may be shy, but they are still powerful creatures.

MYTH: When a black bear stomps its feet and bluffs a charge, it is preparing to attack.

Black bears are territorial toward people and are usually afraid of being attacked themselves. Their most common aggressive displays are merely rituals that they perform when they are nervous. Most likely bears will run away or seek safety in a tree.

Why They Bite

The bite of a black bear is a highly, highly unlikely experience for humans. The greater conflict with humans is the damage the bears can do to your campsite, camping gear, bird feeding station, garden, beehives and more. A friend who lived in bear country always liked to see a summer of good wild berry production. He would always say, "Good berries means the bears are happy." Basically they are eating machines, and they need to put on amazing fat reserves for the upcoming winter. When natural foods such as berries are scarce, bears become bolder and are attracted to our foods and gardens. Unfortunately, this often results in more human/bear conflicts and consequently it means more bruins are killed as "nuisance bears."

THINK TWICE

Think twice about setting up your picnic or camp near garbage cans or other human refuse.

Think twice before trying to get a "cute" photo of a campground bear. Black bears that are used to people cannot be trusted.

How They Bite

Black bears have powerful jaws with a full set of teeth, and sharp, slightly curved claws on each foot. These tools not only help them eat a wide range of foods, but they can serve as weaponry if needed. It should be noted, however, that most bear-related injuries are not major life-threatening episodes.

How Afraid Should I Be?

The likelihood of being on the receiving end of a bear bite is very, very slim. You are far more likely to get killed riding your bicycle or drowning while swimming—and these are considered healthy pastimes.

Interestingly, an average of 1 person is killed in the United States each year by bears of all species. In contrast, white-tailed deer are responsible for more than 175 human deaths each year (deer/car collisions), and dogs kill an average of 15–20 people a year in our country.

The reality is that the media seems to thrive on large animal attacks—while joggers and cyclists who encounter "attacks" from motorists rarely get the same onslaught of news coverage.

Preventing Black Bear Bites

Food is the primary reason that bears and humans encounter each other.

- Keep a clean campsite to minimize bear conflicts. Do not keep food scraps or garbage sitting out, or dump them near your campsite.

- When car camping, close your food containers and keep them in the trunk or inside the vehicle.

- Even if you leave your campsite or picnic table for a short period of time make sure all your food is sealed up. The bottom line is that clean camping will be less likely to attract an unwanted bear to your camp.

- Pack all food in airtight containers or plastic bags to minimize the chance of tempting smells attracting bears.

- Do not camp in an area where there is evidence of bears feeding, such as torn-up logs and ant mounds or signs of bears digging.

- Avoid camping in areas where you find bear droppings, particularly those containing bits and pieces of plastic or paper food packaging.

- If a bear approaches your camp, it is best if you and any others with you can appear as a mob of humans and make noise. This means yelling, banging pots and pans and chasing the bear away. However, keep your distance and allow the bear an escape route.

- In some areas in bear country, it is not unusual to find campsites with bear-proof metal lockers in which to store your food. Properly hanging your food out of reach of bears can also protect it. The U.S. Forest Service recommends that you hang your food at least 12 feet off the ground and 10 feet from the nearest tree trunk.

- Rarely does one come upon a black bear while out hiking. They are usually off and running well before we show up. However, if you encounter one, make your presence known by making noise. This is more effective if there are several people.

Treatment of Bites

If you or someone in your party receives a bear bite or claw scratching, determine the severity of the injury.

- Clean all non-life-threatening injuries and seek medical attention. Even if the wound is superficial, it is wise to seek medical assistance in properly cleaning the wound.

- If there is abundant bleeding, apply pressure to the wound and if possible call 911 for medical assistance.

BOTTOM LINE

It is highly unlikely that a black bear will attack you. Humans attack and kill their fellow humans at a rate more than 90,000 times that of bears harming us. Enjoy any sightings of these amazing animals—while staying a safe, non-threatening distance away. Food is the primary reason bears cause human headaches such as tipped over garbage cans or ransacked camps. Keeping a clean yard and campsite will greatly reduce your chances of bear problems.

Glossary

alpha a socially dominant individual; in the case of a wolf pack, the alpha pair is the socially dominant male and female breeding pair (pg. 119)

anaphylactic shock an extreme, often life-threatening, allergic reaction to an antigen (e.g., a bee sting) to which the body has become hypersensitive following an earlier exposure (pg. 8, 56, 63, 67)

anticoagulant having the ability to slow or inhibit the clotting of the blood (pg. 29, 35, 47, 71, 93)

bacterium a member of a large group of single-celled microorganisms that have cell walls but lack specialized structures and a nucleus; some, not all, can cause disease (pg. 23, 71)

barbel a fleshy filament, sometimes resembling a thick whisker, growing from the mouth or snout of a fish (pg. 79, 80)

carnassials the large upper premolar and lower molar teeth of a carnivore, adapted for shearing/cutting flesh (pg. 116, 120)

carnivorous feeds on other animals (pg. 99, 109, 116, 119, 120)

cercaria a free-swimming larval stage of a parasitic fluke (pg. 11, 13)

cephalothorax the fused head and thorax of spiders (pg. 39, 42)

chelicerae a pair of appendages that appear like legs that are found in front of the mouth of spiders and other arachnids, they are usually pincer-like claws (pg. 41)

clitellum a raised band that encircles the body of a worm and some leeches; it is made up of reproductive segments (pg. 69)

communal shared by others of their kind; some birds and fishes share nesting areas in which there can be many nests in close proximity to each other (pg. 79)

compound eyes an eye consisting of many small visual units, typically found in insects and crustaceans such as certain shrimp (pg. 46)

DEET an abbreviation for an insect repellent called di-ethyl-toluamide, a colorless oily liquid with a mild odor. The chemical effectively "blinds" the insect's senses so the biting/feeding instinct is not triggered (pg. 19, 24, 30, 37)

delayed fertilization a significant delay (longer than the minimum time required for sperm to travel to the egg) between copulation and fertilization, used to describe female sperm storage (pg. 73)

dermatitis a condition of the skin in shich it becomes red, swollen and sore, sometimes with small blisters, resulting from irritation of the skin, such as an allergic reaction (pg. 29)

dormant the slowing or suspending of normal physical functions for a period of time, as if in a deep sleep (pg. 107)

dorsal positioned on the upper side or back of an animal or plant (pg. 81, 93)

eastern equine encephalitis a viral disease carried by mosquitoes (pg. 35, 36)

echolocation the location of objects by reflected sound (echo), particularly used by dolphins, whales and bats (pg. 74, 77)

Epipen a combined syringe and needle that injects a single dose of medication to counteract an aphylactic shock (pg. 56, 63, 67)

eradicate to destroy or put an end to

estrus a period of fertility when many female mammals are receptive to sexual intercourse (pg. 113)

exoskeleton a hardened or rigid external body covering found on some invertebrate animals; it provides both support and protection (pg. 28)

fluke a parasitic flatworm that typically has suckers and hooks for attaching to a host in which it can feed (pg. 13)

hemolymph the fluid found in insects and other invertebrates that is similar to blood

hermaphrodite a person or animal that possesses both male and female sex organs or other sexual characteristics; this might be abnormal or, in the case of earthworms, perfectly normal (pg. 69)

hibernation a physical condition of dormancy and inactivity that is an effective strategy for conserving energy during weather extremes such as winter. The metabolism is greatly reduced often resulting in a lower body temperature, slower breathing and reduced heart rate (pg. 73, 85, 123, 124)

host the animal or plant a parasite lives on or in (pg. 69)

human anaplasmosis one of several tick-borne diseases (pg. 21)

hybridize when two species successfully crossbreed (pg. 79)

Jacobson's organ a scent organ, commonly found on the roof of the mouth of snakes and lizards (pg. 94)

lancets a small two-edged knife or blade with a sharp point (pg. 54)

Lyme Disease a bacterial infection caused by the bite of an infected tick (pg. 21, 23, 25)

larvae the immature form of an insect (pg. 17, 21, 27, 28, 33, 46, 47, 51, 59, 111)

metamorphosis the transformation or change from an immature form to a completely different adult form; common in insects (pg. 17)

miracidium the free swimming larval stage of a parasitic fluke after it passes from an egg to its first host. (pg. 11)

neurotoxic the venom of a brown or black widow spider that may cause neurological symptoms (pg. 42)

omnivore an animal or person that eats both plants and animals. (pg. 97, 103, 107, 123, 124)

ovipositor the slender, tubular organ through which a female insect deposits eggs. (pg. 53)

ovulate the release of ova (egg cells) from the ovary (pg. 73)

parasitic gaining nourishment from others (pg. 69)

pectoral related to the chest or breast; pectoral fins arise on the sides of the fish (near its breast) (pg. 81)

pedipalps specialized appendages, resembling legs, which are attached to an arachnid's cephalothorax. In the scorpion, they are pincers and in spiders they are sensory organs. (pg. 39)

Permethrin a synthetic insecticide of the pyrethroid class, used primarily against disease carrying insects. (pg. 39)

pheromone a chemical substance that triggers a natural behavioral response in another member of the same species. (pg. 39, 61)

pupa an insect in its inactive immature form between larva and adult; such as in the chrysalis stage. (pg. 17, 27, 33, 46, 51, 59)

rabies a viral disease that invades the central nervous system of mammals, including humans (pg. 8, 9, 74-76, 98, 109, 110, 116)

schistosomes a parasitic flatworm that needs two hosts to complete its life cycle. The immature stage needs a freshwater snail host and the adult lives in the blood of birds and mammals. (pg. 11)

spirochete a flexible spiral shaped bacterium (pg. 23)

segmented a body consisted of divided into segments of similar parts (pg. 69)

swimmer's itch an allergic reaction caused by the aquatic larval stage of a group of flatworms called "schistosomes" (pg. 11-15)

thorax the middle section of the body of an insect, between the head and the abdomen, bearing the legs and wings.

vasodilator an agent that helps with the opening or dilation of the blood vessels, which decreases blood pressure (pg. 70)

viable capable of living or working successfully, especially under particular environmental conditions

west nile virus mainly contracted through the bite of a mosquito, interfers with central nervous system and causes inflammation of brain tissue (pg. 35)

References

SWIMMER'S ITCH

Schistosome dermatitis (swimmer's itch) Its Cause, Prevention, and Control.

Brochure printed by MN Dept. of Health, Minneapolis, MN . 1966.

www.dpd.cdc.gov/dpdx/HTML/CercarialDermatitis.htm

www.cdc.gov/ncidod/dpd/parasites/cercarialdermatitis/factsht_cercarialdermatitis.htm

www.dnr.state.wi.us/org/water/fhp/lakes/swimitch.htm#Wisconsin

www.hope.edu/academic/biology/faculty/blankespoor/swimitch/faq.html

NO-SEE-UMS

http://en.wikipedia.org/wiki/Ceratopogonidae

www.bugspray.com/article/sandflies.html

http://creatures.ifas.ufl.edu/aquatic/biting_midges.htm

www.aaaskindoctor.com/bugbites.html

Biting Flies. P.G. Koehler and F. M. Oi, University of Florida. Institute of Food and Agricultural Sciences Extension. ENY-220.

Aquatic Entomology. W. Frank McCafferty. Jones and Bartlett Publishing. 1981

TICKS

How Can I Avoid Ticks Carrying Lyme Disease? Lake and Home & Cabin Kit, Second Edition. Produced by the University of Minnesota.

Ticks And What You Can Do About Them. Roger Drummond,Ph.D. Wilderness Press, Berkely. 1990.

Ticks Off! Controlling Ticks That Transmit Lymes Disease on Your Property. Patrick Guilfoile, Ph. D. ForSte Press, Inc. 2004.

Furtive Fauna, A Field Guide to the Creatures Who Live On You. Roger M. Knutson. Penguin Books. 1992.

Evaluation of a tick bite for possible Lyme Disease. University of Minnesota Medical Center www.uptodate.com. Dec. 2006.

Deer Ticks and Lyme Disease on Cape Cod and the Islands. Brochure provided by Barnstable County Dept. of Health and the Environment.

Parenting the Preschooler – What is Lyme Disease?. University Wisconsin Extension. Brochure.

Advanced Topics in Lyme Disease, Diagnostic Hints and Treatment Guidelines for Lyme and other Tick Borne Illnesses. Joseph J. Burrascano Jr., M.D. Managing Lyme Disease. International Lyme and Associated Diseases Society, 15th Edition. Sept. 2005.

www.geocities.com/HotSprings/Oasis/6455/ticks-links.html

http://creatures.ifas.ufl.edu/urban/medical/deer_tick.htm

www.medicinenet.com/lyme_disease/article.htm

www.cdc.gov/ncidod/dvbid/lyme/ld_humandisease_symptoms.htm

www.health.state.mn.us/divs/idepc/diseases/anaplasmosis/basics.html

BLACK FLIES

www.csuchico.edu/~mmarchetti/FRI/simulidae/simulidaebehavior.html

www.csuchico.edu/~mmarchetti/FRI/simulidae/simulidaecomments.html

www.biology.eku.edu/SCHUSTER/bio%20806/diptera.htm

http://ohioline.osu.edu/hyg-fact/2000/2167.html

http://creatures.ifas.ufl.edu/livestock/bfly.htm

Aquatic Entomology. W. Frank McCafferty. Jones and Bartlett Publishing. 1981.

The New Field Book of Freshwater Life. Elsie B. Klots. G. P. Putnam's Sons, New York. 1966.

MOSQUITOES

Spielman, Andrew and D'Antonio, Michael. Mosquito: A Natural History of our Most Persistent and Deadly Foe, New York: Hyperion, 2001.

Weber, Larry, What's Eating You?, Minnesota Conservation Volunteer, July-August, 2001

Matteson, Sumner W., A Bug Besetting Birds, Horses and Humans Alike, Wisconsin Natural Resources, August, 2003.

www.drgreene.com (Treatment of Mosquito Bites)

Schloegel, Lisa M. and Daszak, Peter, Conservation Medicine: Tackling the Root Causes of Emerging Infectious Diseases and Seeking Practical Solutions, Wildlife Tracks, Humane Society of the United States an the HSUS Wildlife Land Trust, Fall, 2004.

National Center for Infectious Diseases: www.cdc.gov

SPIDERS

Spiders of the North Woods. Larry Weber. Northwoods Naturalist Series. Kollath-Stensas Publishing. 2003.

www.earthlife.net/chelicerata/silk.html

www.mayoclinic.com/health/first-aid-spider-bites/FA00048

http://atshq.org/articles/sbadwp.html

http://2g.isg.syssrc.com/non_trauma/spider.htm

http://encarta.msn.com/media_461517683_761566464_-1_1/Spider_Fangs.html

www.washington.edu/burkemuseum/spidermyth/myths/asleep.html

http://spiders.ucr.edu/

DEER AND HORSE FLIES
www.pestproducts.com/bitesandstings.htm#Diptera

Horse and Deer Flies: Biology and Public Health Risk. Catherine A. Hill and John F. MacDonald, Dept. of Entomology, Purdue University. Purdue Extension E-246-W.

Biting Flies. P.G. Koehler and F. M. Oi, University of Florida. Institute of Food and Agricultural Sciences Extension. ENY-220.

Learn to Live With and Respect Horse Flies and Deer Flies. Steve Murphree, Belmont University. The Tennessee Conservationist.

Aquatic Entomology. W. Frank McCafferty. Jones and Bartlett Publishing. 1981.

The New Field Book of Freshwater Life. Elsie B. Klots. G. P. Putnam's Sons, New York. 1966.

HORNETS
Pests of Paradise First Aid and Medical Treatment of Injuries from Hawaii's Animals by Susan Scott and Craig Thomas, M.D. University of Hawaii Press. 2000

www.everettclinic.com/kbase/topic/symptom/insbt/overview.htm

www.ca.uky.edu/entomology/entfacts/ef634.asp

A Guide to Observing Insect Lives. Donald Stokes. Little, Brown and Company. 1983.

http://doyourownpestcontrol.com/yellowjackets.htm

www.ces.ncsu.edu/depts/ent/notes/Urban/horn-yj.htm

http://ohioline.osu.edu/hyg-fact/2000/2077.html

http://en.wikipedia.org/wiki/Bumblebee

PAPER WASPS
Pests of Paradise First Aid and Medical Treatment of Injuries from Hawaii's Animals by Susan Scott and Craig Thomas, M.D. University of Hawaii Press. 2000

www.everettclinic.com/kbase/topic/symptom/insbt/overview.htm

www.ca.uky.edu/entomology/entfacts/ef634.asp

A Guide to Observing Insect Lives. Donald Stokes. Little, Brown and Company. 1983.

http://doyourownpestcontrol.com/yellowjackets.htm

www.ces.ncsu.edu/depts/ent/notes/Urban/horn-yj.htm

http://ohioline.osu.edu/hyg-fact/2000/2077.html

http://en.wikipedia.org/wiki/Bumblebee

YELLOWJACKETS
Pests of Paradise First Aid and Medical Treatment of Injuries from Hawaii's Animals by Susan Scott and Craig Thomas, M.D. University of Hawaii Press. 2000

www.everettclinic.com/kbase/topic/symptom/insbt/overview.htm

www.ca.uky.edu/entomology/entfacts/ef634.asp

A Guide to Observing Insect Lives. Donald Stokes. Little, Brown and Company. 1983.

http://doyourownpestcontrol.com/yellowjackets.htm

www.ces.ncsu.edu/depts/ent/notes/Urban/horn-yj.htm

http://ohioline.osu.edu/hyg-fact/2000/2077.html

http://en.wikipedia.org/wiki/Bumblebee

HONEY BEES/ BUMBLEBEES
www.ebeehoney.com/Pollination.html

www.ext.vt.edu/departments/entomology/factsheets/honeybee.html

Don't Underestimate the Value of Honey Bees! By Eric C. Mussen, Dept. of Entomology, University of California, Davis, CA 95616

Secret Weapons: Defenses of Insects, Spiders, Scorpions, and other Many-Legged Creatures by Thomas Eisner. The Belknap Press of University of Harvard Press. 2005

www.epipen.com

GIANT WATER BUGS
University of Guelph, Pest Diagnostic Clinic. Laboratory Services Division.

The invasion of the giant water bug. Alex Leary, Times Staff Writer © St. Petersburg Times. Published June 21, 2003

www.eduwebs.org/bugs

BATS

Bats in Question. Don E. Wilson. Smithsonian Institution. 1997.

Mammals of the Great Lakes Region. Allen Kurta. The University of Michigan Press. 1995.

www.cdc.gov/ncidod/dvrd/rabies/bats_&_rabies/bats&.htm

www.batcon.org/home/index.asp?idPage=91&idSubPage=62

www.extension.umn.edu/distribution/naturalresources/DD1141.html

www.cdc.gov/ncidod/dbmd/diseaseinfo/histoplasmosis_g.htm

www.gov.ns.ca/natr/wildlife/Nuisance/bats.htm

BULLHEADS

http://links.jstor.org/sici?sici=0030-1299(198906)55%3A2%3C155%3APDAPHB%3E2.0.CO%3B2-W

www.dnr.state.mn.us/snapshots/fish/brownbullhead.html

MUSKIES

www.dnr.state.mn.us/fish/muskellunge/muskie_northern.html

www.muskie.name/muskie-biology-research.htm

SUNFISH

www.dnr.state.mn.us/fish/sunfish/biology.html

www.dnr.state.mn.us/fish/sunfish/index.html

http://en.allexperts.com/q/Wildlife-2507/index_6.htm

RATTLESNAKES

www.dnr.state.wi.us/org/land/er/publications/snakebite.htm

Rattlesnakes. Mary Ann McDonald. Capstone Press Minneapolis.

Natural History of Amphibian and Reptiles of Wisconsin. Richard Carl Vogt. The Milwaukee Public Museum. 1981.

Amphibians and Reptiles Native to Minnesota. Barney Oldfield and John J. Moriarty. University of Minnesota Press. 1994.

Rattlesnake: Portrait of a Predator. Manny Rubio. Smithsonian Institution Press. 1998.

OTHER SNAKES (GARTER, HOGNOSE, BULL, FOX AND WATER)

Natural History of Amphibian and Reptiles of Wisconsin. Richard Carl Vogt. The Milwaukee Public Museum. 1981.

Amphibians and Reptiles Native to Minnesota. Barney Oldfield and John J. Moriarty. University of Minnesota Press. 1994.

SKUNKS
Mammals of the Great Lakes Region. Allen Kurta. The University of Michigan Press. 1995.

www.dnr.state.mn.us/mammals/skunks/index.html

SNAPPING TURTLES
Amphibians and Reptiles of Minnesota by Barney Oldfield and John J. Moriarty. Published by University of Minnesota Press. 1994.

www.tortoisetrust.org/articles/snappers.htm

http://darrennaish.blogspot.com/2006/05/snapping-turtles-part-iii-bite-lunge.html

RACCOONS
Raccoons. Patrick Merrick. The Child's World Publishing. 2007.

Mammals of North America. Victor H. Cahalane. The Macmillan Company. 1947.

Mammals of the Great Lakes Region. Allen Kurta. The University of Michigan Press. 1995.

www.stanleyparkecology.ca/programs/urbanWildlife/conflicts/raccoonBite.php

www.und.nodak.edu/org/ndwild/raccoon.html

http://animaldiversity.ummz.umich.edu/site/accounts/information/Procyon_lotor.html

www.emedicine.com/ent/topic725.htm

COYOTES
Mammals of the Great Lakes Region. Allen Kurta. The University of Michigan Press. 1995.

Mammals of North America. Victor H. Cahalane. The Macmillan Company. 1947.

Don't Get Eaten: The Dangers of Animals that Charge or Attack. Dave Smith. The Mountaineers Books Publishing. 2003.

www.bcadventure.com/adventure/wilderness/animals/coyote.htm

www.michigan.gov/dnr/0,1607,7-153-10369-104991--,00.html

www.desertusa.com/june96/du_cycot.html

GRAY WOLVES
Mammals of North America. Victor H. Cahalane. The Macmillan Company. 1947.

Mammals of the Great Lakes Region. Allen Kurta. The University of Michigan Press. 1995.

The World of the Wolf. Candace Savage. Sierra Club Books. 1996.

The Wolves of Minnesota. L.David Mech, Editor. Voyageur Press. 2000.

The Way of the Wolf. L. David Mech. Voyageur Press. 1991.

Amazing Wolves, Dogs and Foxes. Mary Ling. Alfred A. Knopf. 1991.

Don't Get Eaten - The Dangers of Animals that Charge or Attack. Dave Smith. The Mountaineers Books Publishing. 2003.

www.fws.gov/Midwest/wolf/biology/biologue.htm

www.dnr.state.wi.us/org/land/er/factsheets/mammals/wolf.htm

www.fws.gov/species/species_accounts/bio_gwol.html

BLACK BEARS

Black Bear Seasons of the Wild. Tom Anderson. Voyageur Press. 1991.

Mammals of the Great Lakes Region. Allen Kurta. The University of Michigan Press. 1995.

Don't Get Eaten: The Dangers of Animals that Charge or Attack. Dave Smith. The Mountaineers Books Publishing. 2003.

RABIES

Don't Get Eaten: The Dangers of Animals that Charge or Attack. Dave Smith. The Mountaineers Books Publishing. 2003.

Bats in Question. Don E. Wilson. Smithsonian Institution. 1997.

www.ext.vt.edu/pubs/wildlife/420-036/420-036.html

DOG BITES

www.dogexpert.com/Dog%20Bite%20Statistics/DogBiteStatistics.html

Photo credits by photographer and page number

Cover photos from Shutterstock

Gary D. Alpert: 54 **J.F. Butler:** 46 **David Cappaert:** 51 (paper wasp) **Mark Cassino:** 47 **CDC/PPPO/DMTS/James Gathany:** 21 (wood tick) **Johnny N. Dell:** 51 (yellow jacket) **Derrick Ditchburn:** 51 (bald faced hornet) **Dudley Edmondson:** 91 (bull, garter, hognose) **Dr. Dennis Feely/University of Nebraska Medical Center:** 22, 24 (electron microscope images of deer tick) **Jim Gathany:** 21 (deer tick) **Image Envision/JVPD/ Eric Engbretson/USFWS:** 79 (sunfish) **Bill Lindner Photography:** 79 (bullhead, muskie) **Eddie McGriff/University of Georgia Extension:** 42 **Tom Murray:** 45 (both) **Phil Pellitteri:** 52 (bottom) **Shutterstock:** 4, 5, 6, 11, 13, 17, 27, 29, 30, 33, 36, 39, 42, 45, 52 (top, middle), 56, 59, 62, 65, 69, 76 (both), 87, 94, 97, 107, 110, 116, 119, 123, 126 **Stan Tekiela:** 73, 91 (fox, water), 92, 100, 103 (both)

About the Author

Tom Anderson is a professional naturalist, an award-winning writer and a wildlife expert. For sixteen years he was director of the Lee and Rose Warner Nature Center, which is associated with the Science Museum of Minnesota and is located in Marine on St. Croix, Minnesota.

In addition to his work at the nature center, Tom is a well-known writer and columnist. For nearly 15 years he wrote "Reading Sign," an award-winning column for the *Chisago County Press*. He is also the author of two books, *Learning Nature by a Country Road* and *Black Bear: Seasons in the Wild*, both from Voyageur Press. He is a published poet and was a columnist for the *Midwest Fly Fishing Magazine* and the Science Museum of Minnesota periodical *Encounters*.

Tom has been honored many times for his writing. He was one of 20 Minnesotan artists chosen to participate in the Millennium Journal Project. In 2003 he was awarded the "Best Commentary Award" by The National Association of Interpretation's periodical, *The Legacy*. In 2004 he was runner-up for the "Best Feature" category.

The natural world and our intimate connection to it inspires Tom to write. He lives southwest of North Branch, but he travels often, especially in the far North. He lives with his lovely wife Nancy Conger in the 19th century farmhouse his Swedish great-great grandparents built.

Tom's website is www.aligningwithnature.com